Eat Well
Live Well

TRIPLE TESTED

Eat Well Live Well

TRIPLE TESTED

Whole-food recipes by color for a full spectrum of nutritional benefits

CONTENTS

Eating well
BY COLOR

What we choose to fuel our bodies with not only affects our weight but our whole well-being. A good diet can be transformative: it can make us feel mentally alert and help our bodies function more efficiently and, critically, it helps protect us from the onset of chronic disease.

In first-world countries, we are fortunate to have a steady supply of diverse, fresh food. If anything, we are in more danger of harming ourselves from overconsumption, especially of the wrong types of food. Along with nature's bounty, our shops are filled with many highly processed man-made foods—limiting these in our diet is the key to good health. Keeping a stable, healthy weight is the frontline defense in long-lasting good health. And the upside of a good diet is that weight tends to be stable, or for those that switch to one, by virtue of a better diet, weight is often lost.

As scientists gain more insight into the unique properties of the foods we eat and how these fuel our bodies' nutritional needs and protect us against disease, nutritional guidelines, provided by accredited dietary practitioners and government bodies, shift and change in line with these new findings. A lot of the dietary changes over the years center on the ratio of fat, protein and carbohydrate advisable in the diet. Underpinning all the different dietary advice over the decades, has been one constant mantra: "eat your veggies." Since fruit and vegetables fall into five color groups—orange, purple, green, white, and red—a modern version of this age-old message is "eat the rainbow."

The pigments that give fruit and vegetables their color are called phytochemicals. These substances occur naturally only in plants and are thought to provide health benefits beyond those that essential nutrients can provide. And interestingly, each color group contains a unique set of health benefits. Phytochemicals may act as antioxidants, protect essential nutrients and protect us from cancer-causing substances. By thinking about plant food from a color perspective, we are more likely to consciously focus on eating a diverse range of plant food. And in turn, provide our bodies with the nutrients it needs on a daily basis.

Eating close to nature is the catch-cry for today's modern diet; that is to say, we should be eating more plant-based food. Plant foods include vegetables, fruit, legumes (beans, chickpeas, and lentils), wholegrains, nuts and seeds. Each chapter in this book contains recipes that focus on a single color—eating from each of these chapters will give you the full spectrum of benefits. You might choose a salad-based dish from one chapter to pair with a more protein-rich dish from another color chapter, then finish with a dessert from a third. But as long as your diet carries the rainbow color ethos throughout the day you have a better chance of good health.

ORANGE Carotenoids give orange vegetables and fruit their color. Beta-carotene is converted in the body to vitamin A, a nutrient that protects our vision and immune function, as well as skin and bone health. Orange-colored foods are also associated with high levels of vitamin C.

PURPLE The pigment that gives fruit and vegetables a bluish purple color, is primarily anthocyanins. Studies show a high intake of anthocyanins to have a beneficial effect on cardiovascular health and on reducing cancer risks, as well as keeping the eyes and urinary tract healthy.

GREEN The pigment chlorophyll colors fruit and vegetables green and contains a range of phytochemicals, which include indoles, carotenoids and saponins, all of which have anti-cancer properties. Leafy vegetables are also a good source of folate, vitamin K, potassium and omega-3 fatty acids.

WHITE You might think that no color equates to reduced nutritional benefit. As we've noted, color is important but it's not the only indicator of phytochemical content. In fact, flavonoids, one of the largest group of phytochemicals, are actually colorless. Flavonoids help keep free-radical damage in check.

RED Red fruit and vegetables are colored by the pigment lyopene, a powerful antioxidant that has been associated with a reduced risk of some cancers, especially prostate cancer, and offers protection against heart disease. They also contain flavonoids, which reduce inflammation and have antioxidant properties.

chargrilled zucchini flowers with orange & herb salad

PREP + COOK TIME
25 MINUTES (+ REFRIGERATION)
SERVES 4 AS A STARTER

10 OUNCES BOTTLED GARLIC AND
HERB-MARINATED FETA

1 TEASPOON FINELY GRATED LEMON ZEST

16 SMALL ZUCCHINI FLOWERS WITH
ZUCCHINI ATTACHED

2 TABLESPOONS OLIVE OIL

¼ CUP LOOSELY PACKED FRESH
DILL SPRIGS

8 FRESH CHIVES, SLICED THINLY

¾-INCH PIECE FRESH TURMERIC

ORANGE & HERB SALAD

2 MEDIUM ORANGES

2 TABLESPOONS OLIVE OIL

1 TABLESPOON WHITE BALSAMIC VINEGAR

¼ TEASPOON GROUND TURMERIC

1 TABLESPOON CHOPPED FRESH CHIVES

1 Drain feta over a pitcher or bowl; reserve the garlic cloves and 1 tablespoon of the oil. Place feta in a small food processor bowl with the reserved garlic cloves, reserved oil, and the zest; process until smooth. Spoon mixture into a piping bag fitted with a ½-inch round tip; refrigerate for 1 hour or until firmer.

2 Meanwhile, make orange and herb salad.

3 Remove and discard stamen from center of zucchini flowers. Make a cut halfway up the zucchini to help the center cook. Pipe feta mixture into flowers then gently twist ends to close. Place on a baking sheet; drizzle with oil, and season.

4 Cook zucchini flowers on a heated oiled grill pan (or on a grill or under a broiler) for 2 minutes each side or until zucchini is tender and grill marks appear.

5 Serve zucchini flowers with salad, zest, dill, and chives. Finely grate turmeric over salad; season with freshly ground black pepper.

orange & herb salad Using a zester, remove peel from oranges (or, peel thinly using a vegetable peeler, avoiding the white pith; cut peel into long thin strips). You will need 1 tablespoon orange peel strips for serving. Segment oranges by removing remaining peel thickly so no white pith remains. Cut between membranes, over a bowl to catch any juice, releasing segments. Squeeze membrane to release any juice; you will need 2 tablespoons juice. Place orange segments and juice in a small bowl with oil, vinegar, turmeric, and chives; toss gently to combine. Season to taste.

tips You can roast the zucchini flowers if you prefer. Place on parchment paper–lined baking sheets. Sprinkle with a little panko (Japanese bread crumbs) and finely grated parmesan; roast at 425°F until tender. Or, you can dip the zucchini flowers in a tempura batter and shallow-fry in rice bran oil.

papaya & pickled carrot salad

PREP TIME

30 MINUTES (+ REFRIGERATION)

SERVES 4 AS A SIDE

**YOU MAY NEED TO START THIS RECIPE
A DAY AHEAD.**

1 TEASPOON TOASTED SESAME OIL

2 TABLESPOONS LIME JUICE

1 MEDIUM RED PAPAYA, PEELED, SEEDED,
SLICED THINLY

1 SMALL GREEN PAPAYA, PEELED, SEEDED,
SLICED THINLY

3 MEDIUM NAVEL ORANGES, PEELED, CUT
INTO ¼-INCH SLICES

1 CUP LOOSELY PACKED FRESH CILANTRO
LEAVES

2 TEASPOONS SESAME SEEDS, TOASTED

PICKLED CARROTS

¾ POUND BABY HEIRLOOM CARROTS

⅔ CUP RICE WINE VINEGAR

1½ TABLESPOONS HONEY

1 TEASPOON SEA SALT FLAKES

1 TABLESPOON THINLY SLICED
YOUNG GINGER

2 FRESH LONG RED CHILES, HALVED
LENGTHWISE, SEEDS REMOVED

1 Make pickled carrots.

2 To make dressing, combine oil, juice, and 2 tablespoons of the reserved pickling liquid in a small pitcher or bowl.

3 Arrange both papaya, orange slices, and pickled carrot mixture on a large plate. Drizzle with dressing; sprinkle with cilantro and sesame seeds.

pickled carrots Trim carrot tops, leaving ¾-inch intact. Peel carrots; halve lengthwise. To make pickling liquid, combine vinegar, honey, salt, and ginger in a small bowl. Place carrots and chiles in a small rectangular glass or ceramic dish; add pickling liquid. Carrots should be fully covered by pickling liquid. Cover dish, refrigerate for 8 hours or overnight. Drain carrot mixture over a pitcher or bowl; discard ginger, reserve pickling liquid.

tips Keep remaining pickling liquid in a glass jar in the fridge for up to 2 weeks. Add to salad dressings or drizzle over grilled fish.

serving suggestion Serve with grilled tofu, chicken, or fish.

warm freekeh, sweet potato & carrot salad

PREP + COOK TIME 1 HOUR
SERVES 4

⅓ CUP WHOLE-GRAIN
GREENWHEAT FREEKEH

⅓ CUP EXTRA-VIRGIN OLIVE OIL

1 CLOVE GARLIC, CHOPPED FINELY

1 TEASPOON GROUND CUMIN

1 TEASPOON GROUND SUMAC

¼ TEASPOON WHITE PEPPER

1½ POUNDS SMALL SWEET POTATOES

1 BUNCH BABY CARROTS
(ABOUT ¾–1 POUND)

2 MEDIUM YELLOW ONIONS,
CUT INTO THICK SLICES

1 TEASPOON LEMON JUICE

1 TABLESPOON THINLY SLICED
PRESERVED LEMON ZEST (SEE TIPS)

1 TABLESPOON FRESH FLAT-LEAF PARSLEY

1 Preheat the oven to 350°F. Line a baking sheet with parchment paper.
2 Cook freekeh in a medium saucepan of boiling salted water on medium-low heat for 45 minutes or until tender.
3 Meanwhile, combine 2 tablespoons of the oil, the garlic, cumin, sumac, and pepper in a large bowl; season.
4 Scrub sweet potato and carrots. Cut sweet potato into thick slices; cut larger carrots in half, lengthwise. Add sweet potato, carrot, and onion to spice mixture in bowl; toss to coat. Transfer to prepared baking sheet. Roast vegetables, turning occasionally, for 40 minutes or until tender.
5 Drain freekeh; return to saucepan. Stir in remaining oil, the juice, and half the preserved lemon zest; season to taste.
6 Place freekeh mixture on a platter; top with roast vegetables, remaining preserved lemon zest, and parsley.

tips You can replace freekeh with pearl barley or brown rice. Preserved lemon is available from delicatessens and specialty food shops. Use the peel only. To prepare preserved lemon, remove and discard pulp and squeeze the juice from peel; rinse peel well before slicing thinly.

baked sweet potato with smoky bulgur chili

PREP + COOK TIME 1 HOUR
SERVES 4

- 4 SMALL SWEET POTATOES
- 1 TABLESPOON OLIVE OIL
- 1 LARGE CARROT, CHOPPED FINELY
- 1 MEDIUM YELLOW ONION, CHOPPED FINELY
- 2 CLOVES GARLIC, CRUSHED
- 1 TABLESPOON GROUND CUMIN
- 2 TEASPOONS SMOKED PAPRIKA
- ½ TEASPOON CAYENNE PEPPER
- 1 CAN (14.5 OZ) DICED TOMATOES
- 1½ CUPS WATER
- ½ CUP COARSE BULGUR
- ½ CUP GREEK-STYLE YOGURT
- 2½ OUNCES FETA, CRUMBLED
- 2 TABLESPOONS SUNFLOWER SEEDS, TOASTED
- ⅓ CUP LOOSELY PACKED FRESH CILANTRO LEAVES

1 Preheat the oven to 350°F.

2 Scrub sweet potato; pat dry. Place sweet potato on a baking sheet; pierce all over with a fork. Bake for 45 minutes or until tender.

3 Meanwhile, heat oil in a large frying pan over medium heat; cook carrot and onion, stirring occasionally, for 10 minutes or until onion softens. Add garlic, cumin, paprika, and cayenne; cook, stirring, for 1 minute or until fragrant. Add tomatoes and the water; bring to a simmer. Simmer, uncovered, for 5 minutes. Add bulgur; cook on lowest heat, uncovered, for 5 minutes or until tender and most of the liquid is evaporated.

4 Split sweet potato in half lengthwise. Top with bulgur chili, yogurt, feta, sunflower seeds, and cilantro. Sprinkle with a little extra smoked paprika, if you like.

tip If you are not eating the chili right away, you may need to add a little more water before serving.

make ahead The bulgur chili can be made a day ahead.

chile carrot paneer

PREP + COOK TIME 50 MINUTES
SERVES 4

**2 BUNCHES BABY CARROTS (ABOUT
1¼ POUNDS), TRIMMED**

----

3 MEDIUM FINGERLING POTATOES

----

2 TABLESPOONS OLIVE OIL

**1 MEDIUM YELLOW ONION,
SLICED THINLY**

**2-INCH PIECE FRESH GINGER, GRATED
FINELY**

----

1 CLOVE GARLIC, CRUSHED

**2 FRESH LONG GREEN CHILES,
SLICED THINLY**

----

1 TEASPOON CUMIN SEEDS

----

1 TEASPOON GARAM MASALA

½ TEASPOON GROUND TURMERIC

----

1 MEDIUM YELLOW BELL PEPPER, SLICED

⅓ POUND ORANGE GRAPE TOMATOES

----

2 TABLESPOONS WATER

6½ OUNCES PANEER, SLICED LENGTHWISE

----

2 TEASPOONS NIGELLA SEEDS

----

1 TABLESPOON MICRO CILANTRO

----

1 Scrub carrots and potatoes. Cut potatoes into ½-inch slices. Boil, steam, or microwave carrots and potatoes, separately, until tender; drain.
2 Heat oil in a large deep frying pan or wok over medium heat; cook onion; stirring, for 5 minutes or until softened. Add carrots, potato, ginger, garlic, half the chile, the cumin, garam masala, and turmeric and cook, stirring, for 2 minutes or until fragrant.
3 Stir in bell pepper, tomatoes, and the water; cook, covered, over low heat, stirring occasionally, for 5 minutes or until bell pepper is softened. Stir in paneer; cover, cook for 2 minutes or until paneer is heated through. Season to taste.
4 Serve paneer mixture sprinkled with remaining chile, the nigella seeds, and cilantro.

tips Paneer is a firm, salty Indian cheese and is available in well-stocked supermarkets. If you can't find it, you can use drained feta or tofu. Halve or omit the chile for a mild version.
serving suggestion Serve with steamed brown basmati rice, pappadums, or naan.

spiced red lentil dhal with fried egg & pumpkin naan

PREP + COOK TIME
1 HOUR 15 MINUTES (+ STANDING)
SERVES 4

1½ POUNDS PUMPKIN, PEELED, CUT INTO
¾-INCH CHUNKS

2 TABLESPOONS OLIVE OIL

2 TEASPOONS CUMIN SEEDS

1 TEASPOON CORIANDER SEEDS

1 MEDIUM RED ONION, CHOPPED FINELY

1 MEDIUM CARROT, CHOPPED FINELY

1 BUNCH CILANTRO, LEAVES PICKED,
STEMS CHOPPED

1½-INCH PIECE GINGER, GRATED FINELY

2 CLOVES GARLIC, CRUSHED

2 TEASPOONS YELLOW MUSTARD SEEDS

1 TEASPOON GROUND TURMERIC

¾ CUP RED LENTILS

2 CUPS VEGETABLE STOCK

2 CUPS WATER

1 CINNAMON STICK

4 FREE-RANGE EGGS

PUMPKIN NAAN

2 TEASPOONS DRIED YEAST

½ CUP WARM WATER

2 TEASPOONS UNREFINED SUGAR

2 CUPS ALL-PURPOSE FLOUR

1 TEASPOON SEA SALT FLAKES

½ CUP LOOSELY PACKED FRESH CILANTRO
LEAVES, CHOPPED COARSELY

2 TABLESPOONS OLIVE OIL

1 Preheat the oven to 400°F.

2 Line a baking sheet with parchment paper. Toss pumpkin with half the oil on the prepared baking sheet. Roast for 30 minutes or until tender; cool 5 minutes. Process pumpkin until smooth. Reserve 1 cup pumpkin purée for the naan and 1 cup for the dhal.

3 Make pumpkin naan.

4 Meanwhile, toast cumin and coriander seeds in a large frying pan over medium heat for 1 minute, shaking pan occasionally, or until fragrant. Transfer to a mortar and pestle; pound until ground.

5 Heat remaining oil in same pan over medium-high heat; cook onion and carrot, stirring, for 5 minutes or until soft. Add cilantro stems, ginger, garlic, mustard seeds, turmeric, and ground spices; cook, stirring, for 1 minute or until fragrant. Add lentils, stock, the water, pumpkin purée reserved for dhal, and cinnamon stick; bring to a boil. Reduce heat to medium-low; simmer, partially covered, for 30 minutes.

6 Stir lentil mixture. Make four indents in mixture; crack eggs into indents; cook, covered, for 10 minutes or until eggs are set.

7 Serve dhal with pumpkin naan, some of the cilantro leaves and toasted shredded coconut, lime cheeks, and red pepper flakes, if you like.

pumpkin naan Combine yeast, the water, and sugar in a medium bowl. Let stand for 5 minutes or until foamy. Stir pumpkin purée reserved for naan, flour, and a pinch of the salt flakes into the yeast mixture until a dough forms. Knead dough on a lightly floured surface for 5 minutes or until smooth and elastic. Transfer to a greased bowl; cover with a clean kitchen towel. Stand in a warm place for 30 minutes or until doubled in size. Transfer dough to a floured surface; knead in cilantro. Divide dough into four pieces; roll each piece into an oval, ⅛-inch thick. Sprinkle with a little of the salt flakes. Brush 1 teaspoon of oil on each side of naan. Cook naan, in batches, on a heated grill pan over high heat for 2 minutes each side or until puffed and golden.

make ahead Dhal can be made to the end of step 5 up to 2 days ahead. Dhal, without eggs, is suitable to freeze for up to 3 months.

spicy lentil patties with fiery fruit salsa

PREP + COOK TIME
1 HOUR (+ REFRIGERATION)
SERVES 4

¼ CUP PEARL AND BLACK BARLEY

½ CUP RED LENTILS

1½ CUPS WATER

⅓ CUP OLIVE OIL

---

1 MEDIUM YELLOW ONION, CHOPPED FINELY

---

2 SMALL CARROTS, GRATED COARSELY

---

2 CLOVES GARLIC, CRUSHED

---

1 TABLESPOON TOMATO PASTE

---

2 TEASPOONS GROUND CUMIN

½ TEASPOON CHILE POWDER

⅓ CUP FINELY CHOPPED FRESH FLAT-LEAF PARSLEY

---

1 CUP FRESH BREAD CRUMBS

---

1 EGG, BEATEN LIGHTLY

---

4 PITA POCKETS, GRILLED

---

1 OUNCE RED VEIN SORREL

FIERY FRUIT SALSA

¼ SMALL PINEAPPLE, CORED, SLICED THINLY

½ MEDIUM MANGO, SLICED THINLY

¼ POUND RED AND ORANGE GRAPE TOMATOES, QUARTERED

---

1 TABLESPOON LIME JUICE

---

1 FRESH LONG RED CHILE, SEEDS REMOVED, SLICED THINLY

---

1 Cook barley in a medium saucepan of boiling water, uncovered, for 30 minutes or until tender; drain.

2 Meanwhile, place lentils and the water in a small saucepan over high heat; bring to a boil. Reduce heat to low; simmer, covered, for 12 minutes or until lentils are tender. Drain. Blend half the lentils in a small food processor until smooth. Transfer to a large bowl with remaining lentils.

3 Heat 1 tablespoon of the oil in a large frying pan over medium heat; cook onion and half the carrot, stirring occasionally, for 5 minutes or until softened. Add garlic, paste, cumin, and chile powder; cook, stirring, for 1 minute or until fragrant. Add to lentils in bowl with barley, parsley, bread crumbs, and egg; mix well. Season well. Cover; refrigerate for 1 hour.

4 Make fiery fruit salsa.

5 Shape lentil mixture into eight oval patties. Heat half the remaining oil in a large frying pan over medium heat; cook half the patties for 3 minutes each side or until browned and heated through. Transfer to a plate; cover to keep warm. Repeat with remaining oil and patties.

6 Serve patties with pita, salsa, sorrel, and remaining carrot.

fiery fruit salsa Combine lingredients in a medium bowl; season to taste. Cover; refrigerate until required.

tip If mango is out of season, you can use papaya.

make ahead Pattie mixture can be made to the end of step 3 a day ahead; keep covered in the fridge. Or, after shaping into patties in step 5, freeze in an airtight container separated with plastic wrap for up to 2 months.

orange & fennel trout gravlax

PREP + COOK TIME 45 MINUTES
(+ REFRIGERATION) SERVES 10

**YOU NEED TO START THIS RECIPE AT LEAST
24 HOURS AHEAD.**

1 CUP ROCK SALT

1 CUP GRANULATED SUGAR

5 TEASPOONS FINELY GRATED ORANGE ZEST

2 TEASPOONS CORIANDER SEEDS,
CRUSHED

1 TEASPOON WHITE PEPPERCORNS,
CRUSHED

2½-POUND CENTER-CUT PIECE OCEAN
TROUT FILLET, SKIN-ON, PIN-BONES
REMOVED

⅓ CUP PINE NUTS

1 TABLESPOON FENNEL SEEDS

1½ TABLESPOONS DIJON MUSTARD

4 SPRIGS FRESH DILL

8 OUNCES MINI CUCUMBERS, SLICED
THINLY LENGTHWISE

¾ CUP CRÈME FRAÎCHE

1 OUNCE TROUT ROE

1 OUNCE FLYING FISH ROE (TOBIKO)

CRUNCHY THINGS

1 CUP RICE WINE VINEGAR

2 TABLESPOONS RAW HONEY

2 TEASPOONS FRESH TURMERIC OR
½ TEASPOON GROUND TURMERIC

10 RADISHES, SLICED THINLY

3 SHALLOTS, SLICED THINLY

1 Combine salt, sugar, 2 teaspoons orange zest, and the crushed seeds and peppercorns in a medium bowl. Spread half the salt mixture over the base of a shallow 12 x 16–inch ceramic or glass dish. Place trout, skin-side down, on mixture; cover with remaining salt mixture. Place plastic wrap directly on salt. Place another dish on top; weight down with cans of food. Refrigerate for 24 hours, turning halfway through.

2 Remove trout from dish; discard salt mixture. Brush salt mixture from trout. Place trout on a platter; cover with plastic wrap. Refrigerate until ready to serve.

3 Place pine nuts and fennel seeds in a small frying pan over low heat; stir constantly over for 5 minutes or until pine nuts are golden; cool. Crush coarsely with a mortar and pestle.

4 Make crunchy things.

5 Spread top of trout with mustard, then sprinkle with combined pine nut mixture and remaining 3 teaspoons zest. Cut trout into very thin slices on an angle. Serve trout with dill, crunchy things, cucumber, crème fraîche, and both roe.

crunchy things Bring rice vinegar to a simmer in a small saucepan. Remove from heat; stir in honey until dissolved. Place remaining ingredients in a medium heatproof bowl. Pour over vinegar mixture; toss well to combine. Let stand for 5 minutes; drain.

tips Use a mandoline or V-slicer to thinly slice the radish, shallots, and cucumber. The salmon will keep, covered, in the fridge for up to 1 week.

romesco with fish skewers

PREP + COOK TIME
45 MINUTES (+ COOLING)
SERVES 4

YOU WILL NEED 12 BAMBOO OR METAL
SKEWERS FOR THIS RECIPE. BEFORE USE,
SOAK BAMBOO SKEWERS FOR 30 MINUTES
IN WATER; OIL METAL SKEWERS.

---

2 SMALL RED BELL PEPPERS, QUARTERED

---

3 CLOVES GARLIC, UNPEELED

1¼ POUNDS FIRM WHITE FISH,
CUT INTO 1-INCH PIECES

---

2 TEASPOONS SMOKED PAPRIKA

⅓ CUP OLIVE OIL

---

2 TEASPOONS FINELY GRATED
LEMON ZEST

---

2 TABLESPOONS FINELY CHOPPED
FRESH FLAT-LEAF PARSLEY

---

24 FRESH BAY LEAVES

¼ CUP BLANCHED ALMONDS

---

2 TABLESPOONS LEMON JUICE

---

2 MEDIUM LEMONS, HALVED

---

1 Preheat broiler on high. Place bell peppers, skin-side up, and garlic on a baking sheet. Place under broiler for 15 minutes or until skins are blackened. Transfer to a medium bowl. Cover with plastic wrap; cool.
2 Combine fish with half the paprika, half the oil, the zest, and parsley in a medium bowl; season. Thread fish and bay leaves onto 12 skewers. Place on a baking sheet; cover, refrigerate.
3 Remove and discard skins from bell peppers and garlic. Process bell pepper, garlic, almonds, juice, remaining paprika, and remaining oil until almost smooth. Transfer romesco to a small bowl; season to taste.
4 Cook fish skewers on a heated oiled grill pan (or in a frying pan or under the broiler) over medium-high heat for 4 minutes or until browned all over and cooked through. Cook lemon halves on grill pan for 1 minute or until browned.
5 Serve fish skewers with romesco sauce and lemon halves.

make ahead Romesco can be made a day ahead; keep covered in the fridge.

red lentil & carrot soup with saffron mussels

PREP + COOK TIME 1 HOUR
SERVES 4

2 TABLESPOONS BUTTER

1 TEASPOON GROUND CORIANDER

1 MEDIUM LEEK, SLICED

2 MEDIUM CARROTS, SLICED

1 CUP RED LENTILS, RINSED

4 CUPS LOW-SODIUM VEGETABLE STOCK

3 CUPS WATER

LARGE PINCH SAFFRON THREADS

2 TABLESPOONS FINELY CHOPPED FRESH
CURLY PARSLEY

1 TRIMMED CELERY STICK,
CHOPPED FINELY

2 POUNDS CLEANED BLACK MUSSELS
(SEE TIPS)

1 Heat butter and ground coriander in a large saucepan over medium heat until butter begins to froth. Add leek and carrots; cook, stirring, for 5 minutes or until dark golden.

2 Add lentils; cook, stirring, for 2 minutes. Add 3 cups of the stock and all the water; bring to a boil. Reduce heat to low; simmer, uncovered, for 30 minutes or until lentils are tender.

3 Meanwhile, place saffron, half the parsley, the celery, and remaining stock in a large saucepan; bring to a boil. Add mussels; cook, covered, for 3 minutes or until mussels have opened. Remove from heat.

4 Using a slotted spoon, transfer mussels to a medium bowl. Pour over ¼ cup of the cooking liquid.

5 Strain remaining cooking liquid from mussels into soup; stir until combined. Season to taste. Ladle soup into bowls; top with mussels and remaining parsley. Serve topped with crisp leek, if you like (see tips).

tips Cleaned black mussels are available in bags from some fish shops. If unavailable, remove beards from mussels, scrub and rinse before using. To make crisp leek, trim white part of 1 medium leek; halve lengthwise. Rinse well; pat dry. Cut leek into long thin strips. Heat oil for shallow-frying in a medium saucepan; cook leek, in batches, until browned lightly and crisp. Remove from the pan with a slotted spoon; drain on paper towels.

roast chicken with pumpkin & currant couscous

PREP + COOK TIME
1 HOUR 50 MINUTES (+ STANDING)
SERVES 4

1 MEDIUM ORANGE

3-POUND WHOLE CHICKEN

2 SPRIGS FRESH ROSEMARY

3 TABLESPOONS BUTTER, SOFTENED

1 BUNCH FRESH CILANTRO

2 TEASPOONS GROUND SUMAC

1 TEASPOON GROUND CUMIN

2 TABLESPOONS EXTRA-VIRGIN OLIVE OIL

1½ POUNDS KABOCHA SQUASH, CUT INTO WEDGES

¾ CUP WHOLE-WHEAT COUSCOUS

¼ CUP CURRANTS

¾ CUP BOILING WATER

1 Preheat the oven to 350°F.
2 Using a vegetable peeler, remove peel thinly from orange. Squeeze orange; you will need ⅓ cup juice.
3 Pat chicken dry inside and out with paper towels. Place rosemary sprigs and half the orange peel into cavity of chicken. Tie legs together with kitchen string; place chicken in a medium baking dish. Rub butter over chicken; season. Roast for 1½ hours or until cooked through.
4 Meanwhile, wash cilantro well; drain. Finely chop cilantro stems and roots; reserve leaves. Place stems and roots in a large bowl with sumac, cumin, oil, and pumpkin, then season; toss to coat. Place pumpkin mixture on a parchment paper–lined baking sheet. After chicken has cooked for 40 minutes, bake pumpkin on a separate shelf, with chicken, for 30 minutes or until pumpkin is tender.
5 Combine couscous and currants with the boiling water in a large heatproof bowl; cover, let stand for 5 minutes or until liquid is absorbed, fluffing with a fork occasionally. Season to taste.
6 Spoon couscous mixture over pumpkin; drizzle with juice. Thinly slice 1 tablespoon of the remaining orange peel; sprinkle over couscous mixture. Return to oven; bake for a further 20 minutes or until just starting to develop a crust.
7 Remove chicken from oven; drain off some of the pan juices into a small bowl. Cover chicken loosely with foil; rest for 15 minutes. Discard fat from pan juices; strain remaining juices into a pitcher or bowl. Pour ½ cup over couscous.
8 Serve chicken with pumpkin and couscous; sprinkle with reserved cilantro.

tip You can use a mixture of pumpkin and sweet potato, if you like.
serving suggestion Serve with a green salad or steamed beans or asparagus.

Turmeric chicken with carrot noodles

PREP + COOK TIME
45 MINUTES (+ REFRIGERATION)
SERVES 4

4 CLOVES GARLIC, CHOPPED COARSELY

¾-INCH PIECE FRESH TURMERIC, PEELED, CHOPPED

½ TEASPOON ROCK SALT

¼ CUP CANNED COCONUT MILK

2 TEASPOONS FISH SAUCE

4 X 8-OUNCE CHICKEN BREAST SUPREMES

4 MEDIUM CARROTS, PEELED INTO LONG STRIPS WITH JULIENNE PEELER

3 OUNCES DRIED VERMICELLI NOODLES

½ POUND YELLOW TOMATOES, HALVED

¼ CUP FRIED SHALLOTS

½ CUP LOOSELY PACKED FRESH MINT LEAVES

1 MEDIUM LIME, CUT INTO WEDGES

LIME DRESSING

½ CUP LIME JUICE

¼ CUP FISH SAUCE

2 TABLESPOONS GRATED PALM SUGAR

1½ TEASPOONS SESAME OIL

1 Pound garlic, turmeric and salt with a mortar and pestle to a smooth paste. Stir in coconut milk and fish sauce. Rub all over chicken; place on a plate. Cover; refrigerate for 20 minutes. Preheat the oven to 350°F and line a baking sheet with parchment paper.

2 Heat a large grill pan (or a grill or broiler) over medium-high heat. Cook chicken for 3 minutes each side or until dark grill marks form. Transfer chicken to the prepared baking sheet. Roast chicken for 12 minutes or until just cooked through. Cover to keep warm; let stand for 5 minutes. Slice thickly.

3 Meanwhile, make lime dressing.

4 Place carrot and noodles in a large heatproof bowl; cover with boiling water. Let stand for 1 minute; drain. Refresh carrot and noodles in another bowl of iced water; drain. Transfer to a large bowl. Add tomatoes and dressing; toss gently to combine. Sprinkle with shallots.

5 Serve chicken with mint, lime wedges, and noodle mixture.

lime dressing Stir ingredients in a medium bowl until sugar dissolves.

tips Chicken supremes are the chicken breast and first wing joint attached with the skin; they are available from gourmet chicken shops and some butchers. You may need to order them. You can brown the chicken in a frying pan, if you prefer. Julienne peelers are available at Asian markets and kitchenware shops.

make ahead Chicken can be marinated a day ahead.

shrimp barley risotto with chile

PREP + COOK TIME

1 HOUR 10 MINUTES (+ STANDING)

SERVES 4

4 CUPS VEGETABLE STOCK

½ TEASPOON LOOSELY PACKED SAFFRON THREADS

¼ CUP EXTRA-VIRGIN OLIVE OIL

1 MEDIUM YELLOW ONION, CHOPPED FINELY

2 CLOVES GARLIC, CRUSHED, PLUS 1 GARLIC CLOVE

1 SMALL FENNEL BULB, CHOPPED FINELY

1½ CUPS PEARL BARLEY

2-INCH PIECE ORANGE PEEL

2 POUNDS UNCOOKED SHRIMP

½ FRESH LONG RED CHILE

1 TEASPOON SEA SALT FLAKES

½ POUND ORANGE GRAPE TOMATOES

1 BALL FRESH BUFFALO MOZZARELLA, TORN

8 SPRIGS FRESH CHERVIL

1 Place stock and saffron in a pitcher and let stand for 10 minutes.

2 Heat 1½ tablespoons of the oil in a large saucepan over medium-high heat; cook onion, crushed garlic cloves, and fennel, stirring for 8 minutes or until soft. Add barley and orange peel, cook, stirring, for 1 minute or until coated. Add stock mixture, bring to a boil. Reduce heat to low; simmer, covered, for 20 minutes. Remove lid; simmer, uncovered, for a further 20 minutes or until barley is almost tender.

3 Meanwhile, remove heads from shrimp. Devein shrimp. Cut along the underside of each shrimp through the shell, from head end almost to the tail, not quite cutting all the way through. Open shrimp out slightly.

4 Coarsely chop chile and remaining garlic clove together; sprinkle with the salt and continue to chop until it forms a paste (the salt will help to break down the ingredients). Combine chile garlic paste with remaining oil; brush over flesh side of shrimp.

5 Cook tomatoes on a lightly oiled grill pan (or on a grill or under a broiler) for 5 minutes or until lightly charred and softened. Remove from grill. Wipe grill clean; cook shrimp on grill for 1½ minutes each side or until just cooked through.

6 Serve risotto topped with tomatoes, shrimp, mozzarella, and chervil.

roast pumpkin dip with spiced chickpeas

PREP + COOK TIME 1 HOUR
SERVES 8 AS A STARTER

2 POUNDS PUMPKIN, PEELED, CHOPPED
COARSELY

4 CLOVES GARLIC, UNPEELED

⅓ CUP PLUS 2 TABLESPOONS OLIVE OIL

2 TABLESPOONS TAHINI

2 TABLESPOONS RED WINE VINEGAR

MOUNTAIN BREAD CRISPS

6½ OUNCES WHOLE-GRAIN PITA BREAD

RICE BRAN OIL SPRAY

1 TABLESPOON SWEET PAPRIKA

1 TABLESPOON SESAME SEEDS

SEA SALT FLAKES

CRACKED BLACK PEPPERCORNS

SPICED CHICKPEAS

1 TABLESPOON OLIVE OIL

1 MEDIUM RED ONION, HALVED, SLICED

1 CAN (15 OZ) CHICKPEAS, DRAINED,
RINSED

1 CLOVE GARLIC, SLICED

2 TEASPOONS CUMIN SEEDS

1 TEASPOON GROUND CORIANDER

¼ TEASPOON RED PEPPER FLAKES

1 TABLESPOON POMEGRANATE MOLASSES

1 Preheat the oven to 350°F. Line a large baking sheet with parchment paper.
2 Place pumpkin, garlic, and 2 tablespons oil on the prepared baking sheet, then season; toss well to coat. Roast for 45 minutes or until tender; cool slightly.
3 Meanwhile, make mountain bread crisps and spiced chickpeas.
4 Squeeze garlic from skins into a food processor. Add roasted pumpkin, tahini, remaining ½ cup oil, and vinegar; process until smooth. Season to taste.
5 Spoon pumpkin mixture into a bowl; top with spiced chickpeas. Serve dip with mountain bread crisps.

pita bread crisps Divide half the bread between two baking sheets; spray lightly with oil. Sprinkle with half the paprika and half the seeds; sprinkle lightly with salt and pepper. Bake for 10 minutes or until crisp. Repeat with remaining ingredients.

spiced chickpeas Heat oil in a large frying pan over medium heat; cook onion, stirring occasionally, for 8 minutes or until soft. Add chickpeas and garlic; cook, stirring, for 3 minutes. Stir in spices and chile; cook, stirring, for 1 minute or until fragrant. Stir in molasses; season to taste. Keep warm.

make ahead Recipe can be prepared a day ahead; refrigerate dip and spiced chickpeas separately. Keep mountain bread crisps in an airtight container at room temperature. Reheat pumpkin mixture and spiced chickpeas just before serving.

slow-roasted pork loin with peach & rosemary jelly

PREP + COOK TIME 5 HOURS

SERVES 4

YOU WILL NEED TO START THIS RECIPE A DAY AHEAD.

---

3 POUNDS BONELESS PORK LOIN

1 TABLESPOON COARSE COOKING SALT

2 LARGE YELLOW ONIONS, SLICED THICKLY

4 X 4-INCH SPRIGS FRESH ROSEMARY

4 SMALL SWEET POTATOES, SKIN ON

4 YELLOW PEACHES, HALVED, PITS REMOVED

PEACH & ROSEMARY JELLY

1½ POUNDS YELLOW PEACHES, HALVED, PITS REMOVED, CHOPPED COARSELY

2 RED APPLES, UNPEELED, CHOPPED COARSELY

¼ CUP LEMON JUICE

2 X 4-INCH SPRIGS FRESH ROSEMARY

6 CUPS COLD WATER

2 CUPS SUPERFINE SUGAR

2 TABLESPOONS WHITE WINE VINEGAR

---

1 Make peach and rosemary jelly.

2 Using a small sharp knife, score pork rind crosswise at ¼-inch intervals; rub with salt. Place pork on a plastic wrap–lined baking sheet. Refrigerate overnight, uncovered, to dry pork rind; this helps the rind to crackle.

3 Preheat the oven to 325°F. Place onion in a single layer in the center of a large baking dish; top with rosemary and pork. Roast, uncovered, for 2 hours.

4 Meanwhile, wrap sweet potato in foil; place on a baking sheet. Roast in oven with pork for further 1 hour or until soft. Remove pork from oven; pour off excess fat. Remove sweet potato from oven; cool slightly. When cool enough to handle, halve lengthwise. Scoop flesh into a medium bowl; mash with a fork until smooth. Season with salt and freshly ground black pepper.

5 Increase oven to 475°F and line a baking sheet with parchment paper. Place peaches, cut-side down, on the prepared baking sheet. Return pork to oven with peaches on separate racks; roast for 30 minutes or until pork rind is puffed. Stand pork, loosely covered, in a warm place for 10 minutes before slicing.

6 Serve pork with peaches, sweet potato mash and jelly.

peach & rosemary jelly Combine peaches, apple, juice, rosemary and the water in a large saucepan over medium-high heat; bring to a boil. Reduce heat to medium; simmer, uncovered, for 1 hour or until pulpy. Strain mixture through a large muslin-lined sieve over a large bowl or pitcher; discard solids. You will need 4 cups liquid. Transfer liquid to a clean saucepan; add sugar and stir over medium-high heat until sugar dissolves. Bring to a boil; boil, uncovered, for 25 minutes or until mixture jells when tested (see tips). Remove from heat; let stand for 10 minutes. Skim off any scum from surface; stir in vinegar. Ladle hot jelly into hot sterilized jars (see tips); seal while hot. Stand overnight or until cooled.

tips To test if jelly is ready, drop a teaspoon of jelly onto a chilled saucer; place saucer in the freezer for 2 minutes to cool. Push jelly with your finger; if the mixture wrinkles, it is ready. Jelly will keep for 3 months in a cool dry place; refrigerate after opening. To sterilize jars, lay the jars down in a stockpot with the lids, cover with warm water. Cover the pot with a lid. Bring to a boil over a high heat. Boil the jars for 20 minutes. Remove the jars from the water carefully with tongs and rubber gloved–hands; drain water from jars. Stand jars and lids upright on a wooden board or on a kitchen towel; the water will evaporate quickly.

mango, coconut & passion fruit parfait

PREP + COOK TIME
35 MINUTES (+ FREEZING)
SERVES 8

**YOU WILL NEED TO MAKE THIS RECIPE
A DAY AHEAD.**

1 MEDIUM RIPE MANGO, CHOPPED,
PLUS 1 MEDIUM MANGO, SLICED THINLY

7 PASSION FRUIT

½ CUP SUPERFINE SUGAR

¼ CUP WATER

5 EGG YOLKS

½ CUP CANNED COCONUT CREAM

¾ CUP CRÈME FRAÎCHE

1 Grease a 4 x 8–inch loaf pan; line base and two long sides with parchment paper, extending the paper 2 inches over the sides.
2 Blend or process chopped mango until smooth; pour into loaf pan. Freeze for 2 hours or until firm.
3 Stir together pulp from 4 passion fruit, the sugar, and the water in a small saucepan over low heat until sugar dissolves; bring to a boil. Reduce heat; simmer, uncovered, for 5 minutes or until syrup is reduced by half.
4 Beat egg yolks in a small bowl with an electric mixer until pale and creamy. With motor operating, gradually add hot passion fruit syrup. Continue beating for 3 minutes or until mixture has cooled. Fold in coconut cream and crème fraîche. Pour passion fruit mixture into loaf pan. Cover; freeze overnight or until firm.
5 To serve, invert parfait onto a platter. Top with mango slices and pulp from the remaining 3 passion fruit.

make ahead Parfait can be made a week ahead.

They are a rich source of vital antioxidants, vitamin A, and fiber

The yellow-orange colored flesh of squash is a clue to its high beta-carotene content. This important antioxidant is converted to vitamin A by the body and is regarded as useful in preventing degenerative diseases and beneficial to good eye health, as it helps maintain the health of the cornea. Pepitas (pumpkin seeds) are a good-quality protein, providing all of the essential amino acids, making them a particularly valuable food source for vegetarians. They are also an excellent source of magnesium, an important mineral that is a catalyst for many biochemical reactions within the body that are required for a healthy immune system.

A world of squash

Buff-skinned and pear-shaped, butternut squash has dense, dry, sweet flesh making it the most versatile of all for cooking. Large and hard-skinned Queensland blue, is a favorite, puréed for scones. Dumpling, golden nugget, and other walled-types are good stuffed. Japanese squash has different varieties, such as kabocha. The green/grey skin cuts easily and is deliciously edible when roasted or chargrilled in wedges.

Vitamin A, which is found in abundance in squash, requires fat for absorption. To gain the benefits team it with extra-virgin olive oil.

THREE EASY WAYS TO USE LEFTOVER ROASTED SQUASH

Combine in a salad with shaved brussels sprouts, red onion, and toasted cashews. Spread squash on grainy rolls, layer with shaved fennel, a large sautéed mushroom, and blue cheese; grill until warmed. Make an instant dip by blending squash, with canned white beans and a little miso.

To roast seeds from a squash or pumpkin, first boil them in salted water for 10 minutes; drain and pat dry. Toss with olive oil and tamari (or salt), roast at 325°F for 15 minutes or until golden.

Lemony squash soup & seeds

Quarter 2 lbs kabocha squash, place with 2 halved garlic bulbs in a roasting pan; sprinkle with 1 teaspoon each smoked paprika, ground cumin, and coriander; drizzle with olive oil. Roast at 400°F for 45 minutes, until tender. Cook 1 sliced onion in olive oil until soft; squeeze garlic into the pan, add squash scooped from skins and 4 cups vegetable stock. Simmer 15 minutes, then purée with an immersion blender. Thin with extra vegetable stock, if necessary. Stir in juice and grated zest of 1 lemon; serve with toasted pepitas.

sweet potato pancakes with grilled peaches & coconut caramel

PREP + COOK TIME
1 HOUR 30 MINUTES (+ COOLING)
SERVES 6 (MAKES 12 PANCAKES)

2 SMALL SWEET POTATOES

¾ CUP WHITE SELF-RISING FLOUR

⅓ CUP WHOLE-WHEAT SELF-RISING FLOUR

1 TEASPOON BAKING SODA

1 TEASPOON GROUND GINGER

⅓ CUP FIRMLY PACKED BROWN SUGAR

1¼ CUPS BUTTERMILK

2 EGGS

2 TABLESPOONS BUTTER, MELTED

1 TEASPOON VANILLA EXTRACT

3 RIPE YELLOW PEACHES, CUT INTO CHEEKS

⅓ CUP PASSION FRUIT PULP

⅓ CUP GREEK-STYLE VANILLA YOGURT

COCONUT CARAMEL

⅓ CUP FIRMLY PACKED BROWN SUGAR

⅓ CUP CANNED COCONUT CREAM

½ TEASPOON SEA SALT FLAKES

1 Preheat the oven to 400°F. Wrap sweet potato in foil; place on a baking sheet. Bake for 50 minutes or until soft. When cool enough to handle, peel sweet potato; mash flesh in a small bowl with a fork until smooth. Cool.
2 Make coconut caramel.
3 Sift flours, soda, and ginger into a large bowl; return husks to bowl. Stir in sugar.
4 Combine mashed sweet potato, buttermilk, eggs, two-thirds of the butter, and the vanilla in a large pitcher or bowl with a spout. Add sweet potato mixture to dry ingredients; stir until combined.
5 Place 1 teaspoon of the remaining butter in a large nonstick frying pan over medium heat; brush evenly over pan surface. Pour ¼ cups of the batter into pan; cook for 3 minutes or until bubbles appear on the surface. Turn pancakes; cook for a further 2 minutes or until browned. Stack pancakes on a plate; cover to keep warm. Brush pan with remaining butter between batches; repeat with remaining batter.
6 Heat a grill pan (or grill) over medium heat. Line plate with parchment paper (don't have any paper near the edge of the plate as it will catch fire); cook peaches for 1½ minutes each side or until softened and grill marks form.
7 Serve pancakes with peaches, coconut caramel, passion fruit and yogurt.
coconut caramel Combine sugar and coconut cream in a small saucepan; bring to a boil. Reduce heat; simmer, uncovered, for 5 minutes or until reduced by one-third. Stir in salt.

tips This is a great recipe for using up leftover roast sweet potato. You will need about 3 passion fruit for this recipe.

no-bake squash pies

PREP + COOK TIME
40 MINUTES (+ REFRIGERATION)
SERVES 6

¾ CUP PECANS

9 FRESH DATES, PITTED

2 TABLESPOONS COCONUT OIL, MELTED

½ TEASPOON GROUND GINGER

SQUASH FILLING

1½ POUNDS KABOCHA SQUASH
PEELED, CHOPPED COARSELY

½ CUP RICOTTA

8 FRESH DATES, PITTED

2 TEASPOONS VANILLA EXTRACT

½ TEASPOON GROUND GINGER

¼ TEASPOON GROUND CINNAMON

1 Process ½ cup of the pecans, 6 of the dates, the oil, and ginger until finely chopped and sticky. Press pecan mixture into the base of six ¾-cup glass jars. Refrigerate until required.
2 Make squash filling.
3 Spoon filling into jars; cover, refrigerate for 2 hours or overnight.
4 Coarsely chop remaining pecans and remaining dates; sprinkle mixture on pies before serving.
squash filling Steam squash for 15 minutes or until soft; drain well. Cool slightly. Process squash with remaining ingredients until smooth.

tip You can use the end of a rolling pin to press the base mixture into the jars.
make ahead Pies can be made to the end of step 3, up to 2 days ahead.

caramelized persimmon & sweet polenta tarts

PREP + COOK TIME
35 MINUTES (+ REFRIGERATION)
MAKES 8

1½ TABLESPOONS COCONUT OIL, MELTED

---

1 CUP MILK

---

1 CUP WATER

¼ CUP HONEY

½ TEASPOON PLUS A PINCH GROUND
CARDAMOM

⅔ CUP POLENTA

---

2 TABLESPOONS NATURAL FLAKED
ALMONDS, TOASTED

---

1 CUP GREEK-STYLE YOGURT

CARAMELIZED PERSIMMONS

---

4 FIRM PERSIMMONS,
CUT INTO THICK WEDGES

---

2 TABLESPOONS HONEY

---

1 TABLESPOON COCONUT OIL, MELTED

---

1 TEASPOON ORANGE BLOSSOM WATER

---

1 TEASPOON LEMON JUICE

---

1 Brush eight 3½-inch round flan molds with removable bottoms with 2 teaspoons of the coconut oil. Place on a large baking sheet.
2 Combine milk, the water, honey, and ½ teaspoon cardamom in a small saucepan; bring to a boil. Gradually whisk in polenta, whisking constantly. Reduce heat to medium; cook, stirring, for 2 minutes or until polenta is thick. Spread polenta over base of flan molds. Refrigerate for 30 minutes.
3 Meanwhile, preheat the oven to 475°F; make caramelized persimmons.
4 Preheat broiler on high. Remove polenta bases from molds; place on a baking sheet. Brush tops with remaining coconut oil. Place under broiler for 3 minutes or until tarts are golden.
5 Top polenta tarts with persimmon and the juices, and almonds. Serve tarts with yogurt topped with a pinch of cardamom.
caramelized persimmons Line a rimmed baking sheet with parchment paper. Place persimmons, cut-side up, on the prepared baking sheet. Combine honey, oil, orange blossom water, and juice in a small bowl; spoon over persimmons. Bake for 15 minutes or until tender and golden.

tip If persimmons are not available, you can use peaches, nectarines, apricots or plums instead.
make ahead You can make the polenta bases a day ahead and refrigerate in an airtight container until required. Heat under the grill just before serving.

ginger & orange filo tart

PREP + COOK TIME
45 MINUTES (+ COOLING)
SERVES 6

RICE BRAN OIL SPRAY

2 SHEETS FILO PASTRY

1 MEDIUM GRAPEFRUIT

3 SMALL NAVEL OR BLOOD ORANGES

¼ CUP COCONUT SUGAR

¾ CUP CRÈME FRAÎCHE

½ CUP FINELY CHOPPED GLACÉ GINGER

FRESH MINT, TO SERVE

1 Preheat the oven to 350°F. Lightly spray an 7- or 8-inch frying pan or skillet with oil.
2 Stack filo sheets, spraying with oil between each layer. Cut in half crosswise to form two squares; stack squares. Gently crumple pastry; line base and side of pan with pastry. Bake for 15 minutes or until golden brown. Cool.
3 Preheat broiler on high.
4 Using a sharp knife, remove peel and all the white pith from grapefruit and oranges. Cut fruit into ½-inch-thick slices. Place slices on a baking sheet and sprinkle with sugar. Place under broiler for 4 minutes or until slices are caramelized and bubbling. Transfer slices to a wire rack to cool. Reserve caramel on a baking sheet.
5 Combine crème fraîche and ginger in a small bowl.
6 Spoon crème fraîche mixture into pastry case; top with fruit slices, caramel, and mint.

make ahead The filo case can be made a day ahead; store in an airtight container at room temperature.

sweet potato cake with candied orange slices

PREP + COOK TIME
3 HOURS (+ COOLING)
SERVES 12

1½ POUNDS SWEET POTATOES, PEELED, CUT INTO ¾-INCH PIECES

1 CUP CHOPPED DRIED APRICOTS

½ CUP UNSWEETENED ORANGE JUICE

1¼ CUP FIRM RICOTTA

¼ CUP MAPLE SYRUP

⅔ CUP LIGHT AGAVE SYRUP

1 CUP BUTTERMILK

2 EGG YOLKS

2 TEASPOONS VANILLA BEAN PASTE

2½ CUPS GROUND ALMONDS

2½ TEASPOONS BAKING POWDER

4 EGG WHITES

1 TABLESPOON HONEY, OPTIONAL

CANDIED ORANGE SLICES

2 MEDIUM ORANGES

¼ CUP HONEY

1 Preheat the oven to 400°F. Line a baking sheet with parchment paper. Place sweet potato pieces on the prepared baking sheet and bake for 30 minutes or until tender; cool.

2 Meanwhile, stir dried apricots and juice in a small saucepan over medium heat for 5 minutes or until apricots have rehydrated and juice has evaporated. Cool.

3 Process ricotta and maple syrup until smooth; transfer to a medium bowl. Cover and refrigerate until required.

4 Reduce oven to 350°F. Grease a deep 9-inch round cake pan; line with three layers of parchment paper.

5 Rinse food processor. Process sweet potato with agave syrup until smooth; transfer to a large bowl. Add apricot mixture; stir in buttermilk, egg yolks, and vanilla paste, then add ground almonds and baking powder.

6 Beat egg whites in a small bowl with an electric mixer until soft peaks form. Gently fold egg whites into cake mixture, in three batches. Spoon mixture into pan; level surface.

7 Bake cake for 1½ hours or until a skewer inserted into the center comes out clean. Cool in pan.

8 Reduce oven to 325°F; make candied orange slices.

9 Remove cake from pan. Spread top and some of the side with ricotta mixture. Top with candied orange slices; drizzle with honey.

candied orange slices Line a large baking sheet with parchment paper. Cut oranges into ⅛-inch-thick slices. Place slices in a single layer on the prepared baking sheet and brush with honey. Bake for 45 minutes or until starting to caramelize. Cool on baking sheet or place some in holes of a mini muffin pan to create curves.

make ahead Cake is best made on day of serving.

superfood spiced pumpkin, carrot & walnut loaf

PREP + COOK TIME
1 HOUR 45 MINUTES
(+ COOLING & STANDING)
SERVES 10

1 POUND PUMPKIN, PEELED, CUT INTO ¾-INCH PIECES

2 TEASPOONS OLIVE OIL

⅓ CUP NATURAL YOGURT

¼ TEASPOON BAKING SODA

2½ OUNCES BUTTER

¼ CUP PURE MAPLE SYRUP

2 EGGS, BEATEN LIGHTLY

1 LARGE CARROT, GRATED COARSELY

1½ CUPS SELF-RISING FLOUR

1 CUP GROUND ALMONDS

½ CUP COARSELY CHOPPED WALNUTS

2 TABLESPOONS WHITE CHIA SEEDS

2 TEASPOONS GROUND CINNAMON

½ TEASPOON GROUND GINGER

¼ TEASPOON GROUND NUTMEG

¼ CUP PEPITAS (PUMPKIN SEEDS)

2 TABLESPOONS PURE MAPLE SYRUP

ORANGE MAPLE RICOTTA

1 CUP RICOTTA

½ TEASPOON FINELY GRATED ORANGE ZEST

1 TABLESPOON PURE MAPLE SYRUP

1 Preheat the oven to 350°F. Line baking shee with parchment paper. Grease a 4 x 8½–inch loaf pan and line the base and long sides with parchment paper.

2 Place pumpkin on the prepared baking sheet, drizzle with oil, and toss to coat. Bake pumpkin for 30 minutes or until tender. Transfer pumpkin to a bowl; mash (or purée in a food processor) until smooth. You will need 1 cup pumpkin purée; cool slightly.

3 Meanwhile, combine yogurt and soda in a glass or ceramic bowl. Let stand for 5 minutes or until yogurt expands.

4 Melt butter and maple syrup in a small saucepan over medium heat until combined; cool 10 minutes.

5 Combine pumpkin purée, egg, and carrot in a medium bowl. Stir in butter mixture then gently fold in yogurt mixture.

6 Combine flour, ground almonds, walnuts, chia seeds, and spices in a large bowl; make a well in the center. Gently fold pumpkin mixture into dry ingredients until just combined. Do not over mix. Spoon mixture into pan; smooth top. Sprinkle with pepitas; cover pan with foil.

7 Bake loaf for 45 minutes. Remove foil; bake for a further 15 minutes or until a skewer inserted into the center comes out clean. Leave loaf in pan for 10 minutes before turning, top-side up, onto a wire rack to cool.

8 Meanwhile, make orange maple ricotta.

9 Serve sliced loaf with orange maple ricotta, drizzled with maple syrup.

orange maple ricotta Process ingredients until smooth.

make ahead Loaf can be made up to 3 days ahead; store in an airtight container. To freeze, slice and wrap individually; freeze for up to 3 months.

grilled eggplant bruschetta with hazelnut skordalia

PREP + COOK TIME 35 MINUTES
SERVES 4

8 BABY EGGPLANTS

¼ CUP OLIVE OIL

1½ TABLESPOONS BALSAMIC VINEGAR

1 TABLESPOON HONEY

14½-OUNCE LOAF SOURDOUGH BREAD

2 TABLESPOONS TRIMMED BABY RED
GARNET LETTUCE

2 TEASPOONS FINELY GRATED
LEMON ZEST

HAZELNUT SKORDALIA

¾ CUP SKINLESS HAZELNUTS

2 LARGE CLOVES GARLIC, CRUSHED

1½ TABLESPOONS LEMON JUICE

2 TEASPOONS RED WINE VINEGAR

¼ CUP OLIVE OIL

¾ CUP WATER

1 Slice each eggplant lengthwise. Brush with 2 tablespoons of the oil on both sides; season. Cook eggplant on a heated grill pan (or on a grill or under a broiler) over medium-high heat for 3 minutes each side or until just cooked through. Transfer to a medium bowl, add vinegar and honey; toss to coat.
2 Cut rounded ends off the bread; reserve for hazelnut skordalia. Cut remaining bread into 8 thick slices; brush with remaining oil. Cook bread on heated grill pan (or on a grill or under a barbecue) for 2 minutes each side or until grill marks appear.
3 Meanwhile, make hazelnut skordalia.
4 Spread skordalia generously onto toasted sourdough; top with eggplant, reserved hazelnuts, red garnet, and zest.
hazelnut skordalia Preheat the oven to 350°F. Spread nuts on a baking sheet. Roast for 8 minutes or until golden brown; cool. Halve ¼ cup of the nuts; reserve for serving. Process remaining nuts until fine crumbs. Add scant ¼ pound of the reserved bread, process until fine crumbs. Add garlic, juice, vinegar, oil, and the water; process until combined. Season to taste.

tip You can use zucchini instead of eggplant and almonds or walnuts instead of hazelnuts, if you like.
make ahead Skordalia can be made up to 1 week ahead; keep in a covered container in the fridge.
serving suggestion For a bite-size version, use a sourdough baguette and cut the eggplant into smaller pieces.

grilled squid & radicchio with kalamata dressing

PREP + COOK TIME
30 MINUTES (+ STANDING)
SERVES 4 (OR 8 AS A STARTER)

2 POUNDS FLOWER-CUT BABY SQUID (SEE TIPS)

2 TABLESPOONS OLIVE OIL

1 TABLESPOON FINELY GRATED LEMON ZEST

2 CLOVES GARLIC, CRUSHED

1 MEDIUM RADICCHIO, LEAVES SEPARATED

½ CUP KALAMATA OLIVES, PITTED, TORN INTO PIECES

¼ CUP SMALL FRESH FLAT-LEAF PARSLEY SPRIGS

2 TABLESPOONS RED AMARANTH LEAVES OR MICRO RED GARNET

KALAMATA DRESSING

2 TABLESPOONS CHOPPED PITTED KALAMATA OLIVES

2 TABLESPOONS OLIVE OIL

2 TABLESPOONS LEMON JUICE

1 Pat squid dry with paper towels. Combine oil, zest, and garlic in a medium bowl, add squid; toss to coat. Season with freshly ground black pepper; let stand for 10 minutes.

2 Meanwhile, make kalamata dressing.

3 Preheat a grill pan (or grill or broiler) over high heat until smoking. Season squid with salt; cook squid for 1½ minutes each side or until charred lightly and just cooked through. Transfer to a plate; cover to keep warm.

4 Serve squid with radicchio and olives; drizzle with dressing and top with parsley and amaranth leaves.

kalamata dressing Blend or process ingredients until smooth. Season to taste.

tips Ask your fishmonger for flower-cut squid with the tentacles attached. If it's not available, clean 3 pounds whole small squid or calamari as usual, leaving the skin and tentacles on. Make four horizontal cuts halfway through the squid hoods. When the squid cooks, it will curve and look like a flower. This recipe is best made close to serving.

grapefruit, asparagus & endive salad

PREP + COOK TIME 30 MINUTES
SERVES 8 AS A SIDE

⅓ CUP PINE NUTS

ABOUT ¾ POUND ASPARAGUS, TRIMMED

4 SMALL RED BELGIAN ENDIVE, LEAVES
SEPARATED

¾ POUND SEEDLESS RED GRAPES, HALVED

1 CUP LOOSELY PACKED FRESH
RED VEIN SORREL LEAVES

1 CUP LOOSELY PACKED FRESH
CHERVIL SPRIGS

¼ CUP LOOSELY PACKED MICRO
PURPLE BASIL LEAVES

GRAPEFRUIT DRESSING

2 LARGE RED GRAPEFRUIT

1 MEDIUM POMEGRANATE

2 SHALLOTS, CHOPPED FINELY

¼ CUP OLIVE OIL

1½ TABLESPOONS RASPBERRY VINEGAR

1 Make grapefruit dressing.
2 Place pine nuts in a small frying pan over medium heat or until browned lightly. Remove from pan; cool.
3 Using a mandoline or V-slicer, shave asparagus into long thin strips (see tips).
4 To serve, layer grapefruit segments with remaining ingredients on a platter; drizzle with dressing. Season with a little salt, if you like.

grapefruit dressing Segment grapefruits, by removing peel thickly so no white pith remains. Cut between membranes, over a bowl to catch any juice, releasing segments; reserve segments in a small bowl for the salad. Squeeze juice from the membrane into bowl; you will need 2 tablespoons juice. To remove the pomegranate seeds, cut pomegranate in half crosswise; hold it, cut-side down, in the palm of your hand over another bowl, then hit the outside firmly with a wooden spoon. The seeds should fall out easily; discard any white pith that falls out with them. Whisk juice, pomegranate seeds, shallots, oil, and vinegar to combine; season to taste.

tips Pine nuts can also be toasted in the oven. Toast on a baking sheet at 350°F for 4 minutes or until browned lightly. If you don't have a mandoline, peel asparagus with a vegetable peeler. It's helpful to peel the asparagus while it's lying on a board to avoid it breaking. Use purple or white asparagus when in season. Small radicchio will work just as well here, however, they are larger than Belgian endive so you would need about two. Blood orange or regular orange can replace grapefruit. The salad is seasoned just before serving with a little vintage merlot salt as it has a wonderful purple hue. You can use regular sea salt flakes instead.

make ahead Salad ingredients and dressing can be prepared ahead; dress the salad just before serving.

serving suggestion This salad is a great side dish. For a main, serve with grilled haloumi, pork, fish, or chicken.

grilled red cabbage with gorgonzola buttermilk dressing

PREP + COOK TIME 30 MINUTES
SERVES 4 AS A SIDE

⅓ CUP PINE NUTS

2½ OUNCES GORGONZOLA CHEESE

½ CUP BUTTERMILK

WHOLE SMALL RED CABBAGE (ABOUT
1½ POUND)

2 TABLESPOONS OLIVE OIL

1 CUP LOOSELY PACKED FRESH
RED VEIN SORREL LEAVES

1 Place pine nuts in a small frying pan over medium heat or until browned lightly. Remove from pan; cool.

2 To make dressing, process gorgonzola and buttermilk until smooth; season to taste.

3 Remove and discard any outer leaves from cabbage; trim core lightly. Cut cabbage in half through the core, then cut each half into four wedges – make sure each wedge is held together by the core. Brush cabbage with oil; season.

4 Cook cabbage on a heated grill pan (or on a grill or under a broiler) over medium heat for 10 minutes each side or until browned and just tender.

5 Place cabbage on a platter. Finely shred any leaves that separate from the wedges and sprinkle over the cabbage. Drizzle with dressing; sprinkle with pine nuts and sorrel.

tips You can also use radicchio or red wombok (napa cabbage). Any toasted nuts can be used. Pine nuts can also be toasted in the oven. Toast on a baking sheet at 350°F for 4 minutes or until browned lightly.

serving suggestion Serve with grilled beef, pork, chicken, or fish.

purple gnocchi with brown butter & hazelnut pangrattato

PREP + COOK TIME
1 HOUR 30 MINUTES
SERVES 4

2 POUNDS PURPLE POTATOES

⅓ CUP ALL-PURPOSE FLOUR

½ CUP FINELY GRATED PARMESAN

2 EGG YOLKS

5 TABLESPOONS BUTTER

2 TABLESPOONS LEMON JUICE

HAZELNUT PANGRATTATO

2 TABLESPOONS OLIVE OIL

⅔ CUP PANKO (JAPANESE BREAD CRUMBS)

⅓ CUP TOASTED HAZELNUTS, SKINNED,
CHOPPED COARSELY

1 TABLESPOON FIRMLY PACKED SAGE
LEAVES, CHOPPED COARSELY

½ TEASPOON FINELY GRATED LEMON ZEST

FRIED SAGE

1 CUP VEGETABLE OIL

⅓ CUP LOOSELY PACKED SAGE LEAVES

1 Preheat the oven to 350°F. Pierce potato skins all over with a skewer; place potatoes on a baking sheet. Bake for 1 hour or until tender.

2 Meanwhile, make hazelnut pangrattato, then fried sage.

3 When potatoes are cool enough to handle; peel skins. Push potato through a ricer or a fine sieve into a large bowl. Add flour, parmesan, and egg yolks to warm potato; season well. Using your hands, mix to a soft dough, taking care not to overwork. Turn dough onto a lightly floured surface; knead lightly until smooth. Divide into four portions. Roll each portion into a ¾-inch thick rope, about 16 inches long. Cut into 1¼-inch pieces; transfer to a lightly floured baking sheet.

4 Cook gnocchi, in batches, uncovered, in a large saucepan of boiling salted water for 2 minutes or until gnocchi float to the surface. Remove gnocchi from pan with a slotted spoon; drain. Transfer to a lightly oiled baking sheet.

5 Melt half the butter in a large shallow frying pan over medium heat for 2 minutes or until browned. Add half the gnocchi; cook for 2 minutes. Add half the juice; cook for a further 1 minute. Wipe out pan with paper towels. Repeat with remaining butter, gnocchi, and juice.

6 Divide gnocchi into bowls. Serve topped with brown butter remaining in pan, pangrattato, and fried sage. Sprinkle with extra lemon zest, if you like.

hazelnut pangrattato Heat oil in a large nonstick frying pan over high heat; cook panko, hazelnuts, and sage, stirring, for 6 minutes or until golden and crisp. Remove pan from heat, stir in zest; season.

fried sage Heat oil in a small saucepan until it reaches 325°F. Pat sage leaves dry with paper towels. Carefully lower sage leaves with tongs or a slotted spoon (oil will bubble fiercely) into hot oil for 20 seconds or until crisp. Remove with slotted spoon; drain on paper towels. Sprinkle with sea salt.

make ahead Gnocchi can be made a day ahead. Store in an airtight container in the fridge. Dust with semolina to prevent sticking, and separate layers with parchment paper. Gnocchi can be frozen for up to 3 months. Cook frozen gnocchi in boiling water for about 3 minutes in step 4.

cheddar & radicchio salad with pickled grapes

PREP + COOK TIME 20 MINUTES
(+ COOLING & REFRIGERATION)
SERVES 4

1½ CUPS RED WINE VINEGAR

⅓ CUP HONEY

2 TEASPOONS CORIANDER SEEDS

4 WHOLE CLOVES

1 CLOVE GARLIC, HALVED

¾ POUND PURPLE SEEDLESS GRAPES,
HALVED

8 RADICCHIO LEAVES, TORN

⅓ CUP LOOSELY PACKED FRESH
FLAT-LEAF PARSLEY LEAVES

4½ OUNCES CHEDDAR, CRUMBLED

⅓ CUP COARSELY CHOPPED
TOASTED WALNUTS

1 TABLESPOON OLIVE OIL

1 Place vinegar, honey, coriander, cloves, and garlic in a small saucepan. Bring to a boil; season.
2 Reserve a handful of the grapes for serving. Place remaining grapes in a clean glass jar. Pour vinegar mixture; seal jar. Cool to room temperature. Refrigerate for at least 4 hours or overnight.
3 Divide radicchio, parsley, cheddar, and walnuts between plates. Drain pickled grapes, reserving 2 tablespoons of the pickling liquid. Top salad with pickled and reserved grapes; drizzle with combined reserved pickling liquid and oil.

tip You can reserve the remaining pickling liquid to use in salad dressings.
make ahead The grapes can be pickled up to a week ahead; store in the fridge.

purple abundance bowl with crisp skin salmon & turmeric dressing

PREP + COOK TIME

1 HOUR 20 MINUTES

SERVES 4

½ CUP WILD RICE, RINSED

4 CUPS WATER

1 TABLESPOON APPLE CIDER VINEGAR

1 TEASPOON RAPADURA SUGAR (SEE TIPS)

¼ TEASPOON PINK SALT

1 MEDIUM BEET, GRATED COARSELY

3 BABY EGGPLANT, CUT INTO ¼-INCH SLICES

2½ TABLESPOONS OLIVE OIL

½ CUP BASMATI RICE, RINSED

4 X 5-OUNCE SALMON FILLETS, SKIN ON

1 TABLESPOON GROUND SUMAC

1 TABLESPOON BLACK SESAME SEEDS

2 CUPS FINELY SHREDDED RED CABBAGE

TURMERIC DRESSING

2 TABLESPOONS TAHINI

2 TABLESPOONS WARM WATER

1½ TABLESPOONS LEMON JUICE

1 TEASPOON HONEY

¼ TEASPOON GROUND TURMERIC

1 Combine wild rice and the water in a medium saucepan over high heat; bring to a boil. Reduce heat to low; simmer, covered, for 30 minutes.

2 Meanwhile, stir vinegar, sugar, and salt in a medium bowl until sugar dissolves. Add beet; toss to coat. Let stand for 30 minutes.

3 Brush eggplant with 2 tablespoons of the oil; season. Cook eggplant, in batches, on a heated grill pan (or under a broiler) over medium heat for 1 minute each side or until browned and tender.

4 Meanwhile, preheat the oven to 400°F.

5 Make turmeric dressing.

6 Add basmati rice to wild rice; cook, covered, for 12 minutes or until rice is tender. Drain.

7 Preheat a medium ovenproof frying pan over medium-high heat. Rub salmon with remaining oil, half the sumac and half the sesame seeds; season. Cook salmon, skin-side down, pressing firmly, for 1 minute. Turn, cook for a further 1 minute. Turn again so that the salmon is skin-side down again; transfer pan to the oven for 5 minutes or until salmon is cooked to your liking.

8 Divide rice mixture, cabbage, beet, eggplant, and salmon between four bowls. Drizzle salmon with turmeric dressing and sprinkle with remaining sumac and sesame seeds.

turmeric dressing Combine ingredients in a small pitcher or bowl; season to taste. Adjust consistency of dressing with a little more warm water, if needed.

tips Rapadura sugar, also known as panela, is an unrefined sugar available from well-stocked supermarkets and health-food stores. You can use any unrefined sugar you prefer If you don't have an ovenproof frying pan, transfer the salmon to a baking sheet.

make ahead Turmeric dressing can be made up to 3 days ahead. Store in a glass jar in the fridge.

fish & black bean blue corn tacos with pickled red onion

PREP + COOK TIME
35 MINUTES (+ STANDING)
SERVES 4

1 CAN (15 OZ) BLACK BEANS, DRAINED, RINSED

⅓ POUND CHERRY TOMATOES, QUARTERED

½ CUP LOOSELY PACKED FRESH CILANTRO LEAVES

2 TABLESPOONS OLIVE OIL

⅔ CUP GREEK-STYLE YOGURT

¼ TEASPOON FINELY GRATED LIME ZEST

1 TABLESPOON LIME JUICE

2 TABLESPOONS RICE FLOUR

¼ TEASPOON CAYENNE PEPPER

1 TEASPOON GROUND CUMIN

1¼ POUNDS FIRM WHITE FISH FILLETS, CUT INTO THICK STRIPS

8 MINI BLUE CORN TORTILLAS

2 CUPS FINELY SHREDDED RED CABBAGE

1 MEDIUM LIME, CUT INTO WEDGES

PICKLED RED ONION

½ CUP WARM WATER

2 TABLESPOONS APPLE CIDER VINEGAR

1 TEASPOON RAPADURA SUGAR (SEE TIPS)

1 SMALL RED ONION, SLICED THINLY

1 Make pickled red onion.
2 Preheat the oven to 350°F.
3 Place beans, tomatoes, cilantro, and half the oil in a medium bowl; toss gently to combine. Season to taste.
4 Combine yogurt, zest, and juice in a small bowl.
5 Combine flour, cayenne, and cumin in a medium bowl; season with salt. Add fish; toss well to coat. Heat remaining oil in a large frying pan over medium-high heat. Cook fish, in batches, for 3 minutes or until golden and just cooked through. Drain on paper towels.
6 Meanwhile, wrap tortillas in foil. Place in oven for 5 minutes or until warm.
7 Divide cabbage, bean mixture, and fish between tortillas; top with pickled onion and yogurt mixture. Serve with lime wedges.

pickled red onion Whisk the water, vinegar, and sugar in a small bowl until sugar dissolves; season with salt. Place onion in a glass jar or bowl. Pour over the pickling liquid. Cover; let stand for at least 1 hour or refrigerate overnight.

tips Rapadura sugar, also known as panela, is an unrefined sugar available at welll-stocked supermarkets and health-food stores. You can use any unrefined sugar you prefer. Ling is called for in this recipe, but any firm white fish fillet will be fine. To give the tortilla an authentic chargrilled flavor, you could heat them, one at a time, on a hot grill pan or in a frying pan or a sandwich press. Blue corn tortillas are available from specialty food stores; you can use white corn tortillas instead if you prefer.

purple carrot & fried eggplant salad with lamb

PREP + COOK TIME
30 MINUTES (+ STANDING)
SERVES 4

2 LAMB LOINS, TRIMMED

⅓ CUP OLIVE OIL

2 MEDIUM RED ONIONS, SLICED THINLY

1¼ POUNDS LEBANESE EGGPLANTS, CHOPPED COARSELY

1¼ POUNDS PURPLE BABY CARROTS, TRIMMED

⅓ CUP COARSELY CHOPPED TAMARI ALMONDS (SEE TIPS)

2½ TABLESPOONS POMEGRANATE MOLASSES

¼ CUP LOOSELY PACKED FRESH BASIL SPRIGS

½ OUNCES RED AMARANTH LEAVES OR MICRO RED GARNET

⅔ CUP HUMMUS

1 Rub lamb with 2 teaspoons of the oil; season.

2 Heat 2 tablespoons of the oil in a large frying pan over medium heat; cook onion, stirring occasionally, for 10 minutes or until caramelized. Transfer to a large bowl.

3 Heat remaining oil in same pan over medium heat; cook eggplant for 5 minutes or until soft and golden. Transfer to same bowl as onion.

4 Meanwhile, add carrots to a large saucepan of boiling salted water; boil, uncovered, until almost tender. Drain. Transfer carrots to same bowl as eggplant and onion, add half the almonds and 2 tablespoons of the pomegranate molasses; toss gently to combine. Season to taste.

5 Heat same cleaned frying pan over high heat; cook lamb for 3 minutes each side or until cooked to your liking. Transfer to a plate; cover loosely with foil, rest for 5 minutes. Slice lamb diagonally.

6 Place carrot salad on a platter; top with lamb, remaining almonds, basil, and amaranth. Serve with hummus drizzled with remaining molasses.

tips You can swap the lamb for beef rump steak, pork fillet, chicken breast fillets, or salmon fillets. Tamari almonds are available from well-stocked supermarkets and specialty nut stands.

steak with purple mash & vincotto beet compote

PREP + COOK TIME 50 MINUTES
SERVES 4

2 POUNDS PURPLE POTATOES, PEELED, CHOPPED COARSELY

2 CLOVES GARLIC, CRUSHED

1 CUP OLIVE OIL

2 X 7-OUNCE BEEF EYE FILLET STEAKS

2 TEASPOONS VINTAGE MERLOT SALT (SEE TIPS)

ABOUT ¾ POUND ASPARAGUS, TRIMMED

½ OUNCE BABY PURPLE KALE LEAVES

VINCOTTO BEET COMPOTE

1 TABLESPOON OLIVE OIL

1 SMALL RED ONION, GRATED

1 TABLESPOON FRESH ROSEMARY LEAVES, CHOPPED FINELY

2 MEDIUM BEETS, PEELED, SLICED THINLY

¾ CUP WATER

½ CUP VINCOTTO (SEE TIPS)

1 Make vincotto beet compote.
2 Meanwhile, place potatoes in a large saucepan of cold salted water; bring to a boil. Cook, covered, for 25 minutes or until soft. Reserve ¼ cup cooking liquid. Drain potatoes. Return potatoes to pan; mash with reserved cooking liquid, garlic, and ¾ cup of the oil until smooth. Season to taste. Return pan to low heat; cover to keep warm.
3 Heat a large frying pan over high heat. Rub steaks all over with 2 tablespoons of the oil; sprinkle steaks with merlot salt. Cook steaks for 3 minutes each side for medium or until cooked to your liking. Transfer to a plate; cover loosely with foil, rest for 5 minutes.
4 Add remaining oil to same frying pan; reduce heat to medium. Cook asparagus for 2 minutes or until tender.
5 Serve sliced steaks with mash, asparagus, beet compote, and kale.
vincotto beet compote Heat oil in a medium saucepan over medium heat; cook onion and rosemary for 2 minutes or until liquid evaporates. Add beet and the water; cook, covered, stirring occasionally, for 10 minutes or until beet is tender. Stir in vincotto; cook, uncovered, stirring occasionally, for another 10 minutes or until thickened. Season to taste. Cool.

tips Vincotto is a sweet-and-sour syrup made from reducing grape must. You can find it in some supermarkets and specialty food stores. If you can't find it, you could use caramelized balsamic vinegar. If the mash has lumps, push it through a medium sieve, in batches, into a bowl with a rubber or silicone spatula. Vintage merlot salt is available from gourmet food stores; you can use sea salt flakes instead.

steamed eggplant with red rice & ginger dressing

PREP + COOK TIME 50 MINUTES
SERVES 4

1 CUP RED RICE

2 CUPS WATER

2 POUNDS BABY PURPLE ASIAN EGGPLANT, HALVED LENGTHWISE

⅓ CUP LOOSELY PACKED PURPLE BASIL OR SHISO LEAVES

2 TABLESPOONS TRIMMED MICRO CILANTRO

2 TABLESPOONS SESAME SEEDS, TOASTED

GINGER DRESSING

¼ CUP WATER

2 TABLESPOONS BROWN SUGAR

¼ CUP FINELY CHOPPED FRESH GINGER

⅓ CUP RICE WINE VINEGAR

2 TEASPOONS SESAME OIL

⅓ CUP PEANUT OIL

1 Make ginger dressing.

2 Wash rice in a sieve; drain well. Place rice in a medium saucepan with the water; bring to a boil. Reduce heat; simmer, covered, for 35 minutes or until tender. Remove from heat; stand, covered, for 10 minutes. Season.

3 Meanwhile, place a large baking paper–lined steamer basket over a large saucepan or wok of simmering water. Steam eggplant, in batches, cut-side down, for 10 minutes or until tender.

4 Serve eggplant on rice, topped with dressing, herbs, and sesame seeds.

ginger dressing Combine ingredients in a small saucepan over high heat; bring to a boil. Boil, uncovered, for 2 minutes or until mixture has reduced by one-third. Remove from heat; season.

tip Red rice has a nutty, earthy flavor and gets its color from a natural pigment in the bran layer, which is high in nutrients. It is available from larger supermarkets, health-food stores, and Asian food stores. It can be served with Thai curries in place of jasmine rice.

pork fillet & slaw with rosemary flatbread

PREP + COOK TIME 45 MINUTES
SERVES 4

⅓ POUND PORK FILLET, TRIMMED

1 TABLESPOON OLIVE OIL

1 CUP WHOLE-WHEAT SELF-RISING FLOUR

1 CUP WHITE SELF-RISING FLOUR

½ TEASPOON SALT

1 CUP GREEK-STYLE YOGURT

2 TEASPOONS WHOLE-GRAIN MUSTARD

⅓ POUND PURPLE GRAPES, HALVED

1 TABLESPOON FRESH ROSEMARY LEAVES

2½ OUNCES FETA IN OIL

½ POUND RED CABBAGE, SHREDDED FINELY

1 Preheat the oven to 425°F. Line two large baking sheets with parchment paper.
2 Brush pork with oil; season. Heat a medium frying pan over high heat; cook pork, covered, for 8 minutes or until well browned all over and just cooked through. Transfer to a plate; cover with foil, rest for 10 minutes.
3 Meanwhile, combine flours and salt in a medium bowl. Make a well in the center; add yogurt and mustard, mix to form a soft dough. Turn onto a lightly floured surface; knead until smooth. Divide dough into four equal portions; roll each portion into a 4¾ x 8–inch oval. Place ovals on prepared baking sheets; top with half the grapes and half the rosemary. Bake for 12 minutes or until golden and risen.
4 Reserve 2 tablespoons of the oil from the feta. Place cabbage, remaining grapes, and remaining rosemary in a medium bowl with reserved oil; toss gently to combine. Season.
5 Serve flatbread topped with feta, slaw, and sliced pork; drizzle with juices on plate from pork. Season with sea salt flakes.

tip The flatbread dough can also be grilled or pan-fried and served with grilled meat, chicken, vegetables, and curries.

Red beets are rich in betalain pigment and orange beets are rich in b-xanthin pigment; both are known for their strong antioxidant, anti-inflammatory, and detoxification properties. Beets are part of a diverse vegetable family, which includes Swiss chard, spinach, and quinoa. Betalains are red and yellow carotenoid pigments, these phytonutrients are important to the nervous system. While betalain pops-up in other foods, the highest concentration is found in beets. Beets also receive kudos as a good source of folate (see below), manganese, potassium, vitamin C, and dietary fiber. It is a low-energy dense food, so it is useful to those trying to control their weight. Research has shown that consuming beets can increase the level of antioxidant enzymes in the body, as well as the number of white blood cells, which are responsible for detecting and eliminating abnormal cells that lead to ill health.

Different shades of beets

This nutritious titan comes in a spectrum of shades and a variety of sizes. From rich purple, white, or golden, to the beautiful red and white rings of chioggia beet. Unless you're using beets in salads, leave the skins on to boil and roast.

To roast, wrap small beets together in foil, or larger ones individually, before placing on a baking sheet. When cool enough to handle, rub off the skins.

Beets lose 25% of their folate when cooked. Folate benefits the brain by slowing down the effects of aging; eat raw to increase nutrient absorption

ONE RAW SALAD
Three delicious uses

Shred ¼ small red cabbage. Combine in a bowl with 2 beets, 1 carrot, and 1 pear, all cut into matchsticks. Whisk ¼ cup olive oil, 1 teaspoon Dijon mustard, 1 teaspoon honey, and 2 tablespoons lemon juice until combined; season, drizzle over salad. Serve scattered with ¼ cup crumbled goat cheese and 1 tablespoon each mint leaves and sunflower seeds. Stuff salad into whole-wheat pita pockets, serve with grilled white fish, or with lamb kebabs. The stems and leaves of beets are also edible: the leaves are rich in vitamins A and C, calcium, and iron. Small leaves can be added to salads, while stems and leaves can be coarsely shredded and sautéed like any other leafy green in a little oil with garlic; finish with a squeeze of lemon.

Beet hummus with tops

Trim leaves and stems from one bunch of beets; reserve ½ cup chopped stems and 1 cup chopped leaves. Peel 1 lb beets; chop coarsely. In a food processor, blend beets with ½ cup almond butter, 1 cup drained chickpeas, 1 teaspoon sea salt flakes, 2 tablespoons lemon juice, 2 cloves garlic, and ¼ teaspoon ground cumin until smooth. Cook stems and leaves in a little olive oil until just wilted. Serve dip topped with leaves.

honey baked plums & grapes with sweet ricotta

PREP + COOK TIME 40 MINUTES

SERVES 4

1¼ POUNDS BLOOD PLUMS, HALVED, PITS REMOVED

¾ POUND RED GRAPES, HALVED, SEEDS REMOVED

---

1 TABLESPOON HONEY

---

4 SPRIGS FRESH THYME

1½ CUPS FULL-FAT RICOTTA

---

2 TABLESPOONS COCONUT SUGAR

½ TEASPOON FINELY GRATED ORANGE ZEST

---

1 Preheat the oven to 400°F. Line a rimmed baking sheet with parchment paper.
2 Place plum halves, cut-side up, and grapes on the prepared baking sheet; drizzle with honey and top with thyme. Bake fruit for 25 minutes or until tender and syrupy.
3 Meanwhile, process ricotta, coconut sugar, and zest until smooth.
4 Serve baked fruit and any juices with ricotta mixture; top with extra orange zest, fresh thyme, and coconut sugar if you like.

tip This dish can be served for brunch or dessert. It also travels well, so it would be great for picnics. Pack the ricotta and fruit separately; keep ricotta cold.

upside-down lemon fig polenta cake

PREP + COOK TIME
1 HOUR 20 MINUTES (+ COOLING)
SERVES 10

1 CUP BUTTER, SOFTENED

1 CUP PLUS 2 TABLESPOONS COCONUT
SUGAR

4 MEDIUM BLACK FIGS, SLICED THICKLY,
PLUS 4 MEDIUM SLICED FIGS

1 TABLESPOON FINELY GRATED
LEMON ZEST

3 EGGS

2½ CUPS GROUND ALMONDS

½ CUP INSTANT POLENTA

1 TEASPOON BAKING POWDER

½ CUP LEMON JUICE

TOFFEE SHARDS

1 CUP POMEGRANATE JUICE

1 CUP SUPERFINE SUGAR

1 Preheat the oven to 350°F. Grease a deep 9-inch round cake pan;
line base and side with parchment paper.
2 Melt 3 tablespoons of the butter in a small saucepan over medium heat;
pour over base of pan, sprinkle with the 2 tablespoons coconut sugar. Arrange
the thickly sliced figs on base, leaving a ½-inch border around edge of pan.
3 Beat remaining butter, zest, and remaining coconut sugar in a small bowl
with an electric mixer until light and fluffy. Add eggs, one at a time, beating
until combined between additions. Fold in ground almonds, polenta, and
baking powder; stir in juice. Spoon mixture over fig in pan; smooth the surface.
4 Bake cake for 1 hour or until a skewer inserted into the center comes out
clean. Leave cake in pan to cool.
5 Meanwhile, make toffee shards.
6 Invert cake onto a plate; decorate with the remaining figs, toffee shards, and
a little extra coconut sugar, if you like.

toffee shards Lightly oil a baking sheet. Stir juice and sugar in a small
saucepan over low heat, without boiling, until sugar dissolves. Bring to a boil;
boil, without stirring, for 8 minutes or until reduced by two-thirds. Pour toffee
onto baking sheet; leave to cool, then break toffee into shards.

make ahead Cake is best made on day of serving. Toffee shards can be made a
day ahead; store between layers of parchment paper in a small airtight
container in a cool, dry place.
serving suggestion Serve with Greek-style or sheep's milk yogurt, ricotta, or
fresh goat's curd.

blueberry & lavender chia puddings with bee pollen

PREP + COOK TIME
10 MINUTES (+ REFRIGERATION)
SERVES 6

2 CUPS UNSWEETENED ALMOND MILK

½ CUP PLUS 2 TABLESPOONS FROZEN
BLUEBERRIES

¼ CUP HONEY

¼ TEASPOON VANILLA POWDER OR
ESSENCE

3 TEASPOONS DRIED LAVENDER

½ CUP WHITE CHIA SEEDS

2 TEASPOONS BEE POLLEN

1 Blend almond milk, the ½ cup blueberries, 1 tablespoon of the honey, the vanilla powder, and 2 teaspoons of the lavender in a high-powered blender until smooth.

2 Pour mixture into a medium bowl; whisk or stir in chia seeds until they are evenly distributed. Pour pudding mixture into six ½-cup glass jars or glasses. Cover; refrigerate for 2 hours or overnight until set.

3 Serve puddings topped with the remaining 2 tablespoons blueberries, the bee pollen, and remaining lavender; drizzle with remaining honey.

tip Bee pollen is available from health food stores.
make ahead Recipe can be made up to 2 days ahead; store covered, in the fridge.

lemon & blackberry cottage cheesecake

PREP + COOK TIME 35 MINUTES
(+ FREEZING & REFRIGERATION)
SERVES 10

**YOU WILL NEED TO BEGIN THIS RECIPE
A DAY AHEAD.**

⅔ CUP SHREDDED COCONUT, TOASTED

1 CUP ALMONDS, TOASTED

¼ CUP COCONUT OIL, MELTED

2 TABLESPOONS COCONUT SYRUP

¼ POUND BLACKBERRIES

1 CUP PURPLE EDIBLE FLOWERS

LEMON BLACKBERRY FILLING

2 MEDIUM LEMONS

2 TABLESPOONS (8 TEASPOONS)
POWDERED GELATIN

¼ CUP COCONUT SYRUP

1 TABLESPOON VANILLA EXTRACT

⅓ POUND BLACKBERRIES
(SEE TIPS)

32 OUNCES COTTAGE CHEESE

½ CUP COCONUT SUGAR

BLACKBERRY SYRUP

⅓ POUND BLACKBERRIES

2 TABLESPOONS COCONUT SYRUP

1 TABLESPOON WATER

1 Grease an 8-inch round springform pan; line base and side with parchment paper.
2 Process ½ cup of the shredded coconut, the almonds, coconut oil, and coconut syrup until finely chopped. Press mixture firmly over base of pan. Freeze for 30 minutes.
3 Meanwhile, make lemon blackberry filling. Pour filling over base; cover, refrigerate overnight or until firm.
4 Make blackberry syrup.
5 Remove cheesecake from pan. Serve cheesecake drizzled with blackberry syrup and topped with blackberries, flowers, and remaining coconut.
lemon blackberry filling Finely grate 2 teaspoons zest from one of the lemons. Squeeze juice from lemons; you need ⅓ cup juice. Place half the juice in a small bowl; sprinkle gelatin over juice. Stir to combine; let stand for 5 minutes. Place remaining juice in a small saucepan with coconut syrup; bring to a boil. Remove from heat. Add gelatin mixture and vanilla; stir until gelatin dissolves. Cool for 5 minutes. Process blackberries until smooth; strain through a medium sieve, discard seeds. Process cheese, blackberry purée, coconut sugar, and zest until smooth. Add gelatin mixture; process until combined.
blackberry syrup Blend or process ingredients in a small blender or processor until smooth.

tips When blackberries are not in season, use frozen berries. Thaw berries, drain, then pat dry with paper towel before using. Use maple syrup if you can't find coconut syrup. Try superfine or light brown sugar instead of coconut sugar. Coconut syrup and sugar are available at well-stocked supermarkets. To toast coconut, place in a frying pan; stir coconut over medium heat until browned lightly. This cheesecake is tangy and not overly-sweet.
make ahead Cheesecake can be made up to 2 days ahead.

poached fruit with coconut crumbs & yogurt

PREP + COOK TIME
35 MINUTES (+ COOLING)
SERVES 6

¼ CUP COCONUT SUGAR

1 VANILLA BEAN, SPLIT LENGTHWISE

2 CUPS WATER

4 MEDIUM GREEN PEARS, PEELED, QUARTERED

1 CUP FROZEN BLACKBERRIES

1 CUP BLUEBERRIES

1 CUP GREEK-STYLE YOGURT

COCONUT CRUMBS

¼ CUP SHREDDED COCONUT

¼ CUP GROUND ALMONDS

2 TABLESPOONS RAW COCOA NIBS

2 TABLESPOONS COCONUT SUGAR

2 TABLESPOONS BLACK CHIA SEEDS

2 TABLESPOONS FLAX SEEDS

2 TABLESPOONS RICE MALT SYRUP

1 Stir coconut sugar, vanilla bean, and the water in a medium saucepan over low heat until sugar dissolves; bring to a boil. Add pears; cook for 10 minutes or until just tender. Add both berries; return to a boil. Transfer fruit to a shallow dish with a slotted spoon.

2 Bring syrup in pan to a boil; boil, uncovered, for 15 minutes or until reduced to ⅓ cup; cool.

3 Meanwhile, make coconut crumbs.

4 Serve fruit and syrup with crumbs and yogurt.

coconut crumbs Preheat the oven to 350°F; line a small baking sheet with parchment paper. Combine coconut, ground almonds, cocoa nibs, coconut sugar, and seeds in a small bowl. Spread mixture over baking sheet; drizzle with syrup. Bake for 5 minutes. Remove from oven; break up with a fork. Return to oven for 10 minutes or until sticky and caramelized. Cool.

tips You can double the crumb recipe and store remaining crumbs in an airtight container. Use as you would a granola for topping yogurts, smoothies, and puddings.

walnut plum puddings

PREP + COOK TIME
45 MINUTES (+ STANDING)
SERVES 6

---

3 SMALL DARK SKINNED, RED-FLESHED
PLUMS, QUARTERED

½ CUP BUTTER, SOFTENED

⅔ CUP RAW SUGAR

---

1 TEASPOON VANILLA BEAN PASTE

---

1 EGG

---

1 CUP FINELY CHOPPED TOASTED WALNUTS

¾ CUP SELF-RISING FLOUR

½ CUP VANILLA YOGURT

SPICED PLUM SYRUP

---

5 SMALL DARK SKINNED, RED FLESHED
PLUMS

⅓ CUP LIGHT AGAVE SYRUP

⅔ CUP WATER

---

1 CINNAMON STICK

---

1 VANILLA BEAN, SPLIT LENGTHWISE

---

1 Preheat the oven to 350°F. Grease a 6-hole Texas (¾-cup) muffin pan; line bases with parchment paper.

2 Blend or process plums until smooth; you will need ¾ cup purée. Beat butter, sugar, and vanilla paste in a small bowl with an electric mixer for 2 minutes or until well combined. Add egg; beat until just combined. Fold in ⅔ cup chopped walnuts and sifted flour, then plum purée. Spoon mixture into pan holes.

3 Bake puddings for 20 minutes or until a skewer inserted into the center comes out clean. Leave puddings in pan for 5 minutes before inverting onto a wire rack.

4 Meanwhile, make spiced plum syrup.

5 Serve puddings warm or at room temperature with plum syrup, yogurt, and remaining ⅓ cup chopped walnuts.

spiced plum syrup Cut 3 of the plums into wedges; reserve in a medium bowl. Coarsely chop remaining plums; place in a small saucepan with agave syrup, the water, cinnamon, and vanilla bean. Bring to a boil. Reduce heat to low; simmer, uncovered, for 8 minutes or until plums are pulpy and sauce is thickened slightly. Let stand for 15 minutes; strain sauce over reserved plums.

tips You can swap walnuts for hazelnuts and agave syrup for honey. Agave syrup can be found in health-food stores and well-stocked supermarkets.

chocolate & beet spiced mud cake

PREP + COOK TIME
1 HOUR 25 MINUTES (+ COOLING)
SERVES 8

4 OUNCES DARK CHOCOLATE
(70% COCOA), CHOPPED

1½ CUPS COCONUT SUGAR

½ CUP COCONUT OIL

4 EGGS, AT ROOM TEMPERATURE,
BEATEN LIGHTLY

½ CUP GROUND ALMONDS

2 CUPS COARSELY GRATED
FRESH BEET (SEE TIP)

1 TEASPOON VANILLA EXTRACT

1¼ CUPS QUINOA FLOUR

2 TABLESPOONS CACAO POWDER

2 TEASPOONS BAKING POWDER

2 TEASPOONS MIXED SPICE

8 OUNCES MASCARPONE

¼ CUP PURE MAPLE SYRUP

CARAMELIZED BABY BEETS

3 BABY BEETS

½ CUP COCONUT SUGAR

1 CUP WATER

1 Preheat the oven to 340°F. Grease a deep 8-inch cake pan; line base with parchment paper.
2 Place chocolate, coconut sugar, and coconut oil in a medium heatproof bowl set over a saucepan of simmering water (don't let base of the bowl touch the water); stir for 3 minutes or until chocolate is melted and mixture is smooth. Remove bowl from pan; let stand for 5 minutes to cool slightly. Stir in eggs, ground almonds, beet, and vanilla.
3 Sift flour, cacao powder, baking powder, and mixed spice into a medium bowl. Gently fold into chocolate mixture. Spoon mixture into pan; level the surface.
4 Bake cake for 50 minutes or until a few crumbs cling to a skewer when inserted into the center of cake. Leave cake in pan for 15 minutes; turn out onto a wire rack to cool.
5 Meanwhile, make caramelized baby beets.
6 Combine mascarpone and maple syrup in a medium bowl. Spread over cooled cake. Top with caramelized baby beets and some of the syrup.
caramelized baby beets Cut each beet into six wedges. Combine sugar and the water in a medium frying pan; stir over low heat, without boiling, until sugar dissolves. Add beet wedges; bring to a boil. Reduce heat; simmer, uncovered, for 10 minutes or until beet is tender.

tip You will need 2 large beets for the cake.
make ahead Uniced cake improves in flavor and texture the day after it is made. It can be made up to 4 days ahead; store in an airtight container.

"super" green frittata

PREP + COOK TIME
1 HOUR 25 MINUTES (+ STANDING)
SERVES 8

2 TEASPOONS OLIVE OIL

¼ CUP GREEN KALE, TRIMMED,
TORN COARSELY

3 OUNCES FRESH MOZZARELLA, TORN

1 TEASPOON FINELY GRATED LIME ZEST

2 LARGE GREEN ZUCCHINI, SLICED THINLY

4 GREEN ONIONS, SLICED THINLY

1 CUP LOOSELY PACKED FRESH
FLAT-LEAF PARSLEY, CHOPPED

⅓ CUP COARSELY CHOPPED FRESH DILL

¾ CUP QUINOA

¾ CUP FINELY GRATED PARMESAN

15 EGGS, BEATEN LIGHTLY

GREEN SAUCE

2 FRESH LONG GREEN CHILES, SEEDS
REMOVED, CHOPPED COARSELY

2 TABLESPOONS PEPITAS (PUMPKIN SEEDS)

1 TABLESPOON LIME JUICE

2½ TABLESPOONS OLIVE OIL

1 Preheat the oven to 350°F. Grease a deep 6-cup round ovenproof dish. Line a baking sheet with parchment paper.
2 Drizzle oil over kale in a large bowl. Massage kale to coat well in oil; this also helps to soften the kale. Spread half the kale over the baking sheet.
3 Add half the mozzarella to remaining kale in bowl, then add remaining ingredients; season, mix well. Transfer mixture to dish; top with remaining mozzarella.
4 Bake frittata for 1 hour or until set; bake kale for 5 minutes or until crisp. Leave frittata in dish for 10 minutes before serving.
5 Meanwhile, make green sauce.
6 Serve frittata topped with roast kale and green sauce. Sprinkle with extra parsley leaves and dill, if you like.
green sauce Process chiles and pepitas in a small food processor until almost combined; the mixture should still have some texture. Transfer to a small bowl or pitcher; add juice and oil, season to taste.

tips Loosely cover dish with foil if the top is becoming too dark. To test if frittata is cooked, insert a thin-bladed knife into the center and withdraw the knife slowly. If the blade is clean, the frittata is cooked. If there is uncooked mixture on the blade, cook for 5 minutes more before testing again.
serving suggestion Serve warm or at room temperature with a tomato salad.

green minestrone with pesto

PREP + COOK TIME 35 MINUTES
SERVES 4

2 TABLESPOONS EXTRA-VIRGIN OLIVE OIL

1 TEASPOON FINELY CHOPPED FRESH SAGE

2 CLOVES GARLIC, CHOPPED FINELY

1 MEDIUM LEEK, CHOPPED FINELY

1 MEDIUM PARSNIP, CUT INTO
½-INCH CUBES

2 TRIMMED CELERY STALKS, SLICED THINLY

4½ OUNCES CURLY KALE, STEMS
DISCARDED, TORN IN PIECES

6 CUPS VEGETABLE STOCK

4½ OUNCES GREEN BEANS, TRIMMED, CUT
INTO ½-INCH LENGTHS

2 MEDIUM ZUCCHINI, HALVED, SLICED
THINLY

1 CAN (15 OZ) CANNELLINI BEANS,
DRAINED, RINSED

PESTO

2 CUPS LOOSELY PACKED FRESH
BASIL LEAVES

⅓ CUP GRATED PARMESAN

¼ CUP PINE NUTS, TOASTED

½ CLOVE GARLIC, PEELED

⅓ CUP OLIVE OIL

1 Heat oil in a large saucepan over medium heat. Cook sage, garlic, and leek, stirring, for 3 minutes or until leek is soft. Cook parsnip, celery, and kale, stirring, for a further 2 minutes or until kale is bright green. Add stock; bring to a boil. Reduce heat to low; simmer, uncovered, for 15 minutes or until parsnip is almost tender.

2 Add green beans, zucchini, and cannellini beans; simmer for a further 5 minutes or until zucchini is just tender. Season to taste.

3 Meanwhile, make pesto.

4 Serve soup topped with pesto.

pesto Blend or process ingredients until smooth. Transfer to a small bowl; season to taste.

tip Cut the leek in half lengthwise and rinse carefully between the layers; they can be quite gritty.

make ahead Soup can be made a day ahead; keep covered in the fridge. Pesto can be made 3 days ahead; keep tightly covered, in a small airtight container, in the fridge. Soup and pesto can be frozen separately, for up to 3 months.

fried green tomatoes with artichokes & white anchovies

PREP + COOK TIME 20 MINUTES
SERVES 4 AS A STARTER

2 EGGS

2 TABLESPOONS FINELY GRATED
PARMESAN

¼ CUP ALL-PURPOSE FLOUR

8 GREEN TOMATOES

⅓ CUP OLIVE OIL

1½ OUNCES BABY ARUGULA

4 MARINATED ARTICHOKES,
HALVED

8 WHITE ANCHOVIES

1 MEDIUM LEMON, CUT INTO WEDGES

¼ CUP LOOSELY PACKED FRESH
BASIL LEAVES

BASIL OIL

½ CUP LOOSELY PACKED FRESH
BASIL LEAVES

½ CUP EXTRA-VIRGIN OLIVE OIL

1 Make basil oil.
2 Whisk eggs and parmesan in a small bowl; season. Place flour into a separate small shallow bowl.
3 Trim top and base of tomatoes. Cut each tomato into two thick rounds.
4 Heat oil in a large frying pan over high heat. Dip cut surfaces of each tomato into flour; tap away excess flour. Dip into egg mixture. Cook tomatoes for 2 minutes each side or until golden. Drain on paper towels.
5 Serve tomato with arugula, artichokes, anchovies, lemon wedges, and a drizzle of basil oil; sprinkle with basil leaves.

basil oil Pour boiling water over basil leaves in a small heatproof bowl; drain immediately. Refresh in another bowl of iced water; drain. Pat basil dry with paper towels. Blend or process basil and oil until smooth. Pour oil through a fine sieve into a small pitcher; discard solids.

tip Green tomatoes are firmer than red tomatoes. If they are not available, you can use firm red vine-ripened tomatoes.

kale & chickpea fritters with smoked salmon

PREP + COOK TIME 35 MINUTES
SERVES 4 AS A MAIN OR 6 AS A
STARTER (MAKES 24 FRITTERS)

½ CUP WHITE QUINOA

1 CUP WATER

4½ OUNCES GREEN KALE, STEMS
DISCARDED, LEAVES CHOPPED

¾ CUP SOUR CREAM

1 TABLESPOON LEMON JUICE

1 CAN (15 OZ) CHICKPEAS, DRAINED,
RINSED

4 EGGS, BEATEN LIGHTLY

2 TABLESPOONS FRESH OREGANO LEAVES

1 TEASPOON GRATED LEMON ZEST

¼ TEASPOON GROUND WHITE PEPPER

VEGETABLE OIL, FOR SHALLOW-FRYING

½ POUND SMOKED SALMON

2 BABY CUCUMBERS, SLICED THINLY

¼ CUP CHOPPED FRESH CHIVES

¼ CUP LOOSELY PACKED BABY KALE LEAVES

1 Rinse quinoa in a sieve; drain. Place quinoa and the water in a small saucepan; bring to a boil. Reduce heat to low-medium; simmer gently for 15 minutes or until most of the water is absorbed. Remove from heat; cover, let stand for 5 minutes. You will need 1 cup cooked quinoa for this recipe.

2 Heat a large nonstick frying pan over medium heat. Cook kale, stirring, for 5 minutes or until kale is wilted and dark green. Transfer to a colander; press to remove any excess liquid. When cool enough to handle, shred kale thinly.

3 Combine sour cream and juice in a small bowl; season.

4 Using a potato masher, coarsely mash chickpeas in a large bowl. Add quinoa and kale, then egg, oregano, zest, and pepper; mix well.

5 Heat oil in a large frying pan; shallow-fry heaped tablespoons of batter, in batches, over medium heat for 2 minutes each side or until golden. Drain on paper towels.

6 Serve fritters topped with salmon, sour cream mixture, cucumber, chives, and baby kale leaves.

tips You can use Swiss chard instead of kale in the fritters. If you can't find baby kale, use baby arugula.

make ahead Batter can be made several hours ahead. Fry just before serving.

green goddess hummus with chargrilled green tomatoes

PREP + COOK TIME 30 MINUTES

SERVES 4

2 X 1½ OUNCES SLICES
WHOLE-WHEAT BREAD

⅓ CUP OLIVE OIL

2 TABLESPOONS FINELY GRATED
PARMESAN

4 SMALL GREEN TOMATOES,
SLICED THICKLY

8 OUNCES BUFFALO MOZZARELLA, TORN
INTO PIECES

2 TABLESPOONS COARSELY CHOPPED
FRESH FLAT-LEAF PARSLEY

1 MEDIUM LEMON, CUT INTO WEDGES

GREEN GODDESS HUMMUS

1 POUND FROZEN FAVA BEANS

1 CLOVE GARLIC, CHOPPED

½ CUP LOOSELY PACKED FRESH
FLAT-LEAF PARSLEY LEAVES

2 TABLESPOONS FRESH TARRAGON LEAVES

2 TABLESPOONS CHOPPED FRESH CHIVES

¼ CUP LEMON JUICE

2 TABLESPOONS TAHINI

¼ CUP OLIVE OIL

2 TABLESPOONS WATER

1 Make green goddess hummus.

2 Process bread until coarse crumbs form. Heat ¼ cup of the oil in a medium frying pan over high heat; cook crumbs, stirring, until toasted and golden. Transfer to a bowl, add parmesan; toss gently to combine.

3 Place tomatoes in a medium bowl with remaining oil; toss well to coat, season well. Cook tomatoes on a heated grill pan (or on a grill or under a broiler) for 2 minutes each side or until browned.

4 Divide hummus between plates. Top with tomatoes, mozzarella, parsley, and crumbs; serve with lemon wedges.

green goddess hummus Cook broad beans in a saucepan of boiling water for 2 minutes or until just tender; drain. Rinse under cold water; drain. Peel broad beans. Process beans with remaining ingredients until smooth. Season to taste.

fried brussels sprouts with blue cheese yogurt

PREP + COOK TIME 35 MINUTES

SERVES 4 AS A STARTER

½ CUP GREEK-STYLE YOGURT

2½ OUNCES BLUE CHEESE, CRUMBLED

½ TEASPOON WHOLE-GRAIN MUSTARD

½ TEASPOON HONEY

1 TEASPOON FINELY GRATED LIME ZEST

2 TEASPOONS FINELY CHOPPED
FRESH CHIVES

2 TEASPOONS FINELY CHOPPED
FRESH MINT

RICE BRAN OIL, FOR SHALLOW-FRYING

2 POUNDS BRUSSELS SPROUTS, TRIMMED,
HALVED

1 Process yogurt, blue cheese, mustard, and honey until smooth. Transfer to a bowl; season to taste.

2 Combine zest and herbs in a small bowl; season.

3 Heat oil in a medium frying-pan over medium-high heat; shallow-fry sprouts, in batches, for 2 minutes or until golden but still green. Drain on paper towels.

4 Place sprouts in a large bowl; sprinkle with herb mixture, then toss to combine. Serve sprouts with blue cheese yogurt for dipping.

tips If you prefer less oil, lightly coat brussels sprouts with cooking oil spray and grill or cook under a broiler. Any blue cheese will work here, and lemon instead of lime is also delicious. If serving as a side dish, drizzle the blue cheese yogurt over the sprouts.

pan-fried gnocchi with green tomato sugo

PREP + COOK TIME
1 HOUR 30 MINUTES
SERVES 4

1 CUP COARSE SALT

3 LARGE RUSSET POTATOES (SEE TIPS)

1 CUP SPELT FLOUR

½ CUP GRATED PARMESAN, PLUS ¼ CUP SHAVED PARMESAN

¼ CUP FIRM RICOTTA, DRAINED WELL

½ CUP FIRMLY PACKED FRESH BASIL LEAVES, CHOPPED FINELY, PLUS ¼ CUP LOOSELY PACKED FRESH BASIL LEAVES

2 OUNCES BABY ARUGULA, CHOPPED FINELY

2 EGG YOLKS

¼ CUP EXTRA-VIRGIN OLIVE OIL

GREEN TOMATO SUGO

1¼ POUNDS GREEN TOMATOES, HALVED

3 CLOVES GARLIC, PEELED

1 FRESH LONG GREEN CHILE, SLICED THINLY

1½ TABLESPOONS OLIVE OIL

1½ TABLESPOONS WHITE BALSAMIC VINEGAR

1½ TABLESPOONS CHOPPED BASIL STALKS

1 TEASPOON RAPADURA SUGAR (SEE TIPS)

1 Preheat the oven to 400°F. Place salt in the center of a medium baking sheet. Pierce potatoes all over with a skewer. Place potatoes on top of salt; bake for 1 hour or until tender.

2 When potatoes are cool enough to handle, peel skins using a small sharp knife. Push potatoes through a sieve or ricer into a large bowl. Sift flour over potato, then add the ½ cup grated parmesan, the ricotta, the ½ cup chopped basil, 1½ ounces arugula, and egg yolks. Mix together to form a soft dough.

3 Turn dough onto a lightly floured surface; divide mixture into eight even portions. Roll each portion into a 6-inch-long, ¾-inch-wide log. Using a floured knife, cut into 1¼-inch pieces. Pinch centers slightly with fingers.

4 Cook gnocchi, in batches, uncovered, in a large saucepan of boiling salted water for 1½ minutes or until gnocchi floats to the surface. Remove gnocchi from pan with a slotted spoon; transfer to a lightly oiled baking sheet. Reserve ½ cup of the cooking water for the sugo.

5 Meanwhile, make green tomato sugo.

6 Heat oil in a large frying pan over medium heat; cook gnocchi, in two batches, for 40 seconds each side or until golden brown.

7 Spoon sugo onto plates, top with gnocchi and the remaining arugula, basil, and the shaved parmesan.

green tomato sugo Preheat the oven to 350°F. Place tomatoes, garlic, and chile in a medium baking dish. Add oil and vinegar; season. Roast for 35 minutes or until caramelized. Pour tomato mixture into a medium saucepan. Add basil stalks, sugar, and reserved pasta cooking water; bring to a boil. Boil, uncovered, for 2 minutes. Using a stick blender, blend until smooth. Season.

tips It is important to make the gnocchi dough while the potato is still hot, as this will give a softer texture. Rapadura sugar, also known as panela, is an unrefined sugar available from well-stocked supermarkets and health-food stores. You can use any unrefined sugar you prefer.

Tuscan kale & ricotta cannelloni

PREP + COOK TIME 35 MINUTES
SERVES 4

- 1 POUND TUSCAN KALE
- ½ POUND BABY SPINACH
- 1 POUND FIRM RICOTTA
- 6½ OUNCES FETA, CRUMBLED
- 1 TEASPOON FINELY GRATED LEMON ZEST
- 2 CLOVES GARLIC, CRUSHED
- ⅔ CUP FROZEN BABY PEAS, THAWED
- ¾ CUP FINELY GRATED PARMESAN
- 2 EGGS, BEATEN LIGHTLY
- 2 TABLESPOONS OLIVE OIL
- ¼ CUP BUTTER, CHOPPED
- ½ CUP WALNUTS, CHOPPED
- 2 TABLESPOONS FRESH THYME LEAVES

1 Preheat the oven to 425°F. Line two baking sheets with parchment paper.
2 Remove stems from the kale; place leaves in a large heatproof bowl. Place spinach in another large heatproof bowl. Pour boiling water over kale and spinach; let stand for 1 minute, drain separately. Refresh in separate bowls of iced water; drain. Squeeze any excess water from kale and spinach.
3 Chop spinach; place in a large bowl. Stir in ricotta, feta, zest, garlic, peas, ½ cup finely grated parmesan, and egg; season.
4 Open kale leaves; overlap two large leaves lying flat. Place 2 tablespoons of the ricotta mixture at one end of leaves; roll up to form "cannelloni." Place cannelloni on prepared baking sheets. Repeat with remaining kale leaves and ricotta mixture to make a total of 20 cannelloni; you may need to use some of the smaller leaves. Sprinkle cannelloni with the remaining ¼ cup parmesan, then drizzle with oil; season with salt.
5 Bake cannelloni for 15 minutes or until crisp and heated through.
6 Meanwhile, heat butter and walnuts in a small frying pan until butter is beginnning to brown. Add thyme; swirl to combine.
7 Serve cannelloni drizzled with butter mixture and a little extra lemon zest, if you like.

make ahead This recipe can be made to the end of step 4 several hours ahead; keep covered in the fridge.
serving suggestion Serve with a tomato and basil salad.

green veggie bibimbap bowls

PREP + COOK TIME 30 MINUTES

SERVES 4

---
1 CUP JASMINE RICE

½ CUP MIXED QUINOA
---
2 CUPS WATER
---
3 TEASPOONS SESAME OIL
---
3 TEASPOONS SOY SAUCE
---
2 CLOVES GARLIC, CRUSHED

½ POUND BROCCOLINI, TRIMMED

½ POUND FROZEN EDAMAME
IN POD, THAWED
---
1 LARGE ZUCCHINI, CUT INTO
THICK MATCHSTICKS
---
2 TABLESPOONS SUNFLOWER OIL
---
4 EGGS
---
3 OUNCES ALFALFA SPROUTS

½ SHEET NORI, SHREDDED FINELY
---
1 TABLESPOON SESAME SEEDS

CHILE DRESSING

¼ CUP RICE WINE VINEGAR
---
2 TABLESPOONS SOY SAUCE
---
3 TEASPOONS GOCHUJANG (SEE TIPS)
---
3 TEASPOONS SUPERFINE SUGAR
---

1 Rinse rice and quinoa in a sieve under cold water until water runs clear; drain well. Place in a medium saucepan with the water; bring to a boil. Reduce heat to low; simmer, covered, for 10 minutes or until holes appear. Remove pan from heat; stand, covered, for 10 minutes.

2 Meanwhile, combine sesame oil, soy sauce, and garlic in a small bowl. Halve broccolini crosswise, then halve thick stems lengthwise; place in a bowl. Shell edamame; place in another bowl. Place zucchini in a third bowl. Divide sauce mixture between vegetables; toss to combine.

3 Heat a wok over high heat. Stir-fry broccolini for 1 minute or until bright green; remove from wok. Stir-fry zucchini for 30 seconds or until it begins to soften; remove from wok. Stir-fry edamame for 30 seconds or until heated through; remove from wok.

4 Make chile dressing.

5 Heat sunflower oil in wok over high heat; cook eggs, one at a time, for 1 minute or until edges are crisp and whites just set.

6 Spoon rice mixture into serving bowls. Top with vegetables, fried egg, and sprouts. Drizzle with dressing; sprinkle with nori and sesame seeds.

chile dressing Whisk ingredients in a small bowl until combined.

tips Gochujang is a Korean chile sauce available from Asian food stores. If unavailable, use sriracha, available from supermarkets. Bibimbap is traditionally served in a hot stone bowl and topped with raw egg which is stirred through the hot rice to cook.

make ahead Dressing can be made 2 days ahead.

avocado, shrimp & asparagus salad

PREP + COOK TIME 35 MINUTES
SERVES 4

⅓ POUND ASPARAGUS,
TRIMMED, HALVED

½ CUP OLIVE OIL

¼ CUP LEMON JUICE

1 SHALLOT, CHOPPED COARSELY

¼ CUP FIRMLY PACKED FRESH
BASIL LEAVES

¾ CUP FIRMLY PACKED FRESH
FLAT-LEAF PARSLEY LEAVES

1 POUND COOKED MEDIUM SHRIMP

1½ OUNCES SNOW PEA TENDRILS

¼ CUP SHELLED PISTACHIOS, TOASTED,
CHOPPED COARSELY

1 LARGE AVOCADO, CUT INTO WEDGES

1 Bring a medium saucepan of water to a boil. Add asparagus; boil for 20 seconds or until bright green. Remove with a slotted spoon; place into a bowl of iced water. Drain well; pat dry. Halve asparagus stems lengthwise.
2 Blend oil, juice, shallot, basil, and ¼ cup parsley in a small blender until smooth; season to taste.
3 Shell and devein shrimp, leaving tails intact. Place snow pea tendrils, pistachios, ¼ cup parsley, the asparagus, shrimp, and half the dressing in a large bowl; toss gently to combine. Serve topped with avocado, remaining dressing and the remaining ¼ cup parsley.

tips The dressing would also be delicious served over grilled chicken, fish, or beef. For a heartier meal, you may wish to use 2 pounds shrimp.
make ahead This recipe is best made close to serving as the lemon juice will discolor the herbs in the dressing.

Turmeric fish with green rice

PREP + COOK TIME 45 MINUTES
SERVES 4

½ TEASPOON CUMIN SEEDS

1 STALK LEMONGRASS, WHITE PART ONLY,
SLICED THINLY

3 CILANTRO STEMS, ROOTS TRIMMED,
LEAVES RESERVED

¾-INCH-PIECE FRESH GINGER, PEELED,
CHOPPED COARSELY

½ TEASPOON GROUND TURMERIC

2 TEASPOONS COCONUT SUGAR

1½ TABLESPOONS FISH SAUCE

2 TEASPOONS COCONUT OIL

1 MEDIUM YELLOW ONION, SLICED THINLY

1⅔ CUPS CANNED COCONUT MILK

2 CUPS FISH STOCK

2 TABLESPOONS LIME JUICE

4 X ¼ POUND SKINLESS WHITE FISH FILLETS

1 FRESH LONG GREEN CHILE, SLICED THINLY

2 TABLESPOONS MICRO CILANTRO

1 MEDIUM LIME, CUT INTO 4 WEDGES

GREEN BASMATI RICE

1 CUP BASMATI RICE, RINSED

4 CUPS WATER

2 TEASPOONS COCONUT OIL

1 CLOVE GARLIC, CRUSHED

¼ POUND BABY SPINACH LEAVES

1 CUP FROZEN PEAS

½ CUP LOOSELY PACKED FRESH CILANTRO
LEAVES

1 Make green basmati rice.
2 Cook cumin seeds in a small frying pan over medium heat, stirring, for 1 minute or until lightly toasted.
3 Using a mortar and pestle, pound lemongrass, cilantro roots, and ginger into a paste. Add turmeric, toasted cumin seeds, coconut sugar, and 1 tablespoon of the fish sauce; pound until well combined.
4 Heat coconut oil in a medium deep frying pan over medium heat; cook the paste, stirring, for 1 minute or until fragrant. Add onion; cook, stirring, for 5 minutes or until soft. Stir in coconut milk, stock and juice. Bring to a boil, then reduce heat immediately to a gentle simmer.
5 Carefully add fish to pan; cover, cook for 8 minutes, or until fish is just cooked through. Stir in remaining fish sauce.
6 Serve fish and sauce on green basmati rice, topped with chile, reserved cilantro leaves, micro cilantro, and lime wedges.

green basmati rice Place rice and the water in a medium saucepan over high heat; bring to a boil. Reduce heat to low; simmer, uncovered, for 12 minutes or until rice is tender. Drain well. Heat coconut oil in same pan over medium heat; cook garlic, stirring, for 1 minute or until fragrant. Add spinach and peas; cook, stirring, for 1 minute or until spinach is wilted. Add cilantro and rice; cook, stirring, until well combined. Season to taste.

tips this recipe calls for snapper, but any white fish fillet will be fine. You can use long-grain rice instead of basmati if you like.

chicken, Tuscan kale & brussels sprouts salad

PREP + COOK TIME
1 HOUR (+ STANDING)
SERVES 4

¾ POUND CHICKEN
BREAST FILLETS

⅓ CUP OLIVE OIL

2 TEASPOONS SESAME SEEDS

2 TEASPOONS NIGELLA SEEDS

1 TEASPOON GROUND TURMERIC

1 TEASPOON GARAM MASALA

½ TEASPOON GROUND WHITE PEPPER

1 TEASPOON SEA SALT

1 POUND BRUSSELS SPROUTS, TRIMMED,
HALVED

½ POUND TUSCAN KALE, TRIMMED,
LEAVES TORN

1 CAN (15 OZ) CHICKPEAS, DRAINED,
RINSED

2 TABLESPOONS TRIMMED MICRO PARSLEY

GREEN SAUCE

1 CUP LOOSELY PACKED FRESH
FLAT-LEAF PARSLEY LEAVES

⅓ CUP LOOSELY PACKED FRESH
MINT LEAVES

1 CLOVE GARLIC, PEELED

1 TABLESPOON DRAINED BABY CAPERS

2 TABLESPOONS LEMON JUICE

⅓ CUP EXTRA-VIRGIN OLIVE OIL

1 Preheat the oven 350°F. Line a large baking sheet with parchment paper.
2 Bring a large saucepan of salted water to a boil. Add chicken; return to a boil. Cover; remove from heat. Let stand for 30 minutes.
3 Meanwhile, combine oil, seeds, spices, and salt in a large bowl. Add brussels sprouts and kale; toss to coat. Place sprouts, cut-side down, on prepared baking sheet. Roast for 40 minutes or until golden. Turn sprouts; add kale to baking sheet. Roast for a further 10 minutes or until tender.
4 Remove chicken from poaching liquid. Cool slightly; shred flesh coarsely.
5 Make green sauce.
6 Arrange brussels sprouts, kale, chickpeas, and chicken on a platter; drizzle with green sauce, and top with micro parsley and extra mint leaves, if you like.
green sauce Process ingredients in a small food processor until smooth. Transfer to a small bowl; season to taste.

tip For a vegetarian version, add grilled haloumi in place of chicken.
make ahead Green sauce can be made up to 2 days ahead; store, tightly covered in a small airtight container, in the fridge.

edamame & wasabi pea soba noodle salad

PREP + COOK TIME 25 MINUTES
SERVES 4

1½ CUPS SHELLED EDAMAME

⅓ POUND GREEN TEA
SOBA NOODLES

1 LARGE AVOCADO, CHOPPED

¾ POUND SHREDDED COOKED CHICKEN

½ CUP FIRMLY PACKED FRESH CILANTRO
LEAVES

2 GREEN ONIONS, SLICED THINLY

⅓ CUP WASABI PEAS

MISO DRESSING

2 TABLESPOONS WHITE (SHIRO)
MISO PASTE

1 TABLESPOON HONEY

¼ CUP APPLE CIDER VINEGAR

2 TABLESPOONS OLIVE OIL

2 TEASPOONS GRATED FRESH GINGER

1 TEASPOON WASABI PASTE

1 Make miso dressing.
2 Cook edamame in a saucepan of boiling water for 2 minutes; remove with a slotted spoon. Rinse under cold water.
3 Add noodles to same pan of boiling water; cook for 4 minutes or until noodles are just tender. Drain.
4 Place noodles in a large bowl with edamame, avocado, chicken, cilantro, green onion, half the wasabi peas, and the dressing; toss gently to combine. Serve topped with remaining wasabi peas.
miso dressing Place ingredients in a screw-top jar; shake well. Season to taste.

tip This recipe uses premixed wasabi paste in a tube, which is milder than powdered or fresh wasabi.
make ahead Assemble this salad just before serving.

the botanist bowl

PREP + COOK TIME 50 MINUTES
SERVES 4

---

4 CUPS CHICKEN STOCK

1 TEASPOON WHOLE BLACK PEPPERCORNS

1 BAY LEAF

**2 X ½ POUND CHICKEN
BREAST FILLETS**

⅛ POUND BRUSSELS SPROUTS, HALVED

2 TABLESPOONS OLIVE OIL

**½ POUND GREEN KALE, STEMS DISCARDED,
SHREDDED FINELY**

1 MEDIUM AVOCADO, CUT INTO WEDGES

**2 TABLESPOONS TOASTED ALMONDS,
CHOPPED COARSELY**

SUPERFOOD PESTO

**½ CUP FIRMLY PACKED FRESH
BASIL LEAVES**

**½ CUP FINELY CHOPPED GREEN KALE
LEAVES**

¼ CUP TOASTED ALMONDS

¼ CUP FINELY GRATED PARMESAN

2 TEASPOONS LEMON JUICE

1 SMALL CLOVE GARLIC, PEELED

⅓ CUP EXTRA-VIRGIN OLIVE OIL

1 TEASPOON SPIRULINA

1 Preheat the oven to 400°F. Line a baking sheet with parchment paper.
2 Place stock, peppercorns and bay leaf in a medium saucepan over medium heat. Add chicken; if chicken is not covered in stock, add a little water. Bring to a boil; reduce heat to low, simmer, uncovered, for 4 minutes. Cover pan, turn off heat; let stand for 30 minutes.
3 Meanwhile, place brussels sprouts on the prepared baking sheet, drizzle with half the oil; toss to coat. Turn sprouts cut-side up; season. Roast for 20 minutes or until crisp and golden.
4 Make superfood pesto.
5 Place kale and remaining oil in a large bowl; season with sea salt. Using your hands, rub oil and salt into kale until kale softens.
6 Remove chicken from the poaching liquid; shred coarsely.
7 Divide kale between bowls; top with brussels sprouts, chicken, avocado, almonds, and pesto.

superfood pesto Process basil, kale, almonds, parmesan, juice, and garlic until finely chopped. With motor operating, gradually add oil in a thin, steady stream; process until smooth. Stir in spirulina; season to taste.

make ahead Pesto can be made up to 4 days ahead. Store, tightly covered, in a small airtight container in the fridge.

Kale is one of the most nutritious veggies and is particularly rich in carotenoids.

Carotenoids in kale can be converted to vitamin A in the body. It is also one of the best sources of other carotenoids, lutein, and zeaxanthin, these are known for the essential role they play in eye health. Kale is terrific for vitamin C, vitamin K, vitamin B6, calcium, potassium, copper, and manganese, and supplies good levels of several B group vitamins, including, folate, iron, magnesium, and phosphorus. With such a spectrum of nutrients, it's no wonder it has become a darling of nutritionists, and deservedly so.

kale pesto

In a small food processor, blend ½ cup torn kale with ½ cup finely grated parmesan, ¼ cup firmly packed fresh flat-leaf parsley, 1 clove crushed garlic, 1 teaspoon finely grated lemon zest, 1 tablespoon lemon juice, and 2 tablespoons extra-virgin olive oil until a coarse paste forms. Season. Toss pesto with 4 oz spelt or whole-wheat spaghettini with ¼ teaspoon red pepper flakes.

One cup of kale provides over 200% of your daily-recommended amount of vitamin A and 100% of your daily-recommended vitamin C.

KALE AND OTHER CRUCIFEROUS VEGETABLES

Broccoli, brussels sprouts, cabbage, and cauliflower contain compounds called thiocyanates which can interfere with the body's ability to absorb iodine. People with thyroid problems should avoid eating large quantities. It should also be noted that juicing these vegetables contributes to a massive intake of these compounds.

HOW TO COOK AND PREPARE

In addition to nutrients, versatility is the other thing kale has in spades. Name another leafy green that can be roasted to delicious crispness? There isn't one. For all uses, strip the leaves from the tough stems. Eaten raw, unless shredded finely, its coarse texture requires a fair bit of chewing. But for salads there's a trick to render it to textural perfection. Tear into a bowl, scatter lightly with salt and drizzle with 1 tablespoon olive oil. With your hands, massage oil and salt into the leaves until softened and glossy. From there, you can sauté it or stir it into curries and soups.

miso chicken & stir-fried greens

PREP + COOK TIME 15 MINUTES
SERVES 4

4 GREEN ONIONS

1 POUND BROCCOLINI OR GAIL LAN, TRIMMED

2 TABLESPOONS SUNFLOWER OIL

2 CLOVES GARLIC, CHOPPED FINELY

¾-INCH-PIECE FRESH GINGER, CHOPPED FINELY

½ POUND GROUND CHICKEN

2 TABLESPOONS COOKING SAKE

1 TABLESPOON MISO PASTE

1 TABLESPOON HONEY

2 TEASPOONS SESAME OIL

½ POUND GREEN BEANS, TRIMMED

6½ OUNCES FROZEN EDAMAME BEANS IN POD, THAWED, SHELLED

2 TEASPOONS TOASTED SESAME SEEDS

1 FRESH LONG RED CHILE, SLICED THINLY

1 Coarsely chop the white part of the green onions; cut green part into long thin strips. Separate gai lan leaves from stems; cut thick stems in half lengthwise.

2 Heat half the sunflower oil in a large wok over high heat; stir-fry white part of onion, garlic, and ginger for 30 seconds or until fragrant. Add chicken; stir-fry, breaking up lumps, for 2 minutes or until browned lightly.

3 Combine sake, miso paste, honey, and sesame oil in a small bowl or pitcher. Add to chicken mixture; stir-fry for 2 minutes. Remove from wok; cover to keep warm.

4 Heat remaining sunflower oil in wok over high heat; stir-fry beans for 1 minute or until skin starts to wrinkle in some patches. Add gai lan stems and edamame; stir-fry for 1 minute or until stems are almost tender. Add gai lan leaves; stir-fry for 30 seconds or until just wilted.

5 Arrange greens on a large platter. Top with chicken mixture; drizzle with cooking liquid. Sprinkle with green part of onion, seeds, and chile.

tip Ground pork can be used in place of chicken, or make it vegetarian with some finely chopped firm tofu or tempeh.

green masala chicken curry

PREP + COOK TIME 50 MINUTES
SERVES 4

2 BUNCHES FRESH CILANTRO, ROOTS,
STEMS AND LEAVES CHOPPED COARSELY

1 CUP LOOSELY PACKED FRESH
MINT LEAVES

¼ POUND BABY SPINACH LEAVES, PLUS
1½ OUNCES BABY SPINACH LEAVES

1 FRESH JALAPEÑO CHILE, SEEDS
REMOVED, CHOPPED COARSELY

4 CLOVES GARLIC, CHOPPED

¼ CUP LEMON JUICE

½ CUP WATER

2 TABLESPOONS OLIVE OIL

1 MEDIUM YELLOW ONION,
SLICED THICKLY

8 SMALL SKINLESS BONELESS CHICKEN
THIGH FILLETS (ABOUT 2½ POUNDS TOTAL)

1½ TEASPOONS GROUND TURMERIC

½ TEASPOON GROUND CINNAMON

½ TEASPOON GROUND CARDAMOM

¼ TEASPOON GROUND CLOVES

1 CUP CANNED COCONUT CREAM

⅓ CUP NATURAL FLAKED ALMONDS,
TOASTED

1 MEDIUM LIME, CUT INTO WEDGES

1 Reserve a handful of cilantro leaves and mint leaves for serving. Blend or process remaining cilantro and mint with ¼ pound spinach, the chile, garlic, juice, and the water until smooth.
2 Heat oil in a large deep frying pan over medium-high heat; cook onion, stirring, for 5 minutes or until starting to brown. Add chicken; cook for 5 minutes or until chicken is browned on both sides. Add spices; cook, stirring, for 1 minute or until fragrant.
3 Stir in cilantro purée and coconut cream; bring to a boil. Reduce heat to low; simmer, uncovered, for 20 minutes or until sauce thickens slightly and chicken is cooked through. Season to taste.
4 Serve curry topped with the remaining 1½ ounces spinach leaves, the reserved cilantro and mint, and the almonds and lime wedges.

tip This is a great sauce for a vegetable curry. In step 3, add chunky chopped vegetables such as pumpkin, potato, sweet potato, or cauliflower and drained and rinsed chickpeas or lentils. Simmer until vegetables are tender.
serving suggestion Serve with steamed brown or basmati rice or pappadums.

sweet & sour catalan Swiss chard with rosemary lamb

PREP + COOK TIME
45 MINUTES (+ REFRIGERATION)
SERVES 4

2 TABLESPOONS COARSELY CHOPPED
FRESH ROSEMARY

1 CLOVE GARLIC, CRUSHED

⅓ CUP OLIVE OIL

12 FRENCH-TRIMMED LAMB CUTLETS

3 GREEN ONIONS, SLICED THICKLY, PLUS 2
GREEN ONIONS, SLICED THINLY

⅓ CUP SHERRY VINEGAR

2 SPRIGS FRESH THYME

2 TABLESPOONS HONEY

¼ CUP CURRANTS

1 POUND SWISS CHARD, TRIMMED

¼ CUP TOASTED PINE NUTS

1 Combine rosemary, garlic, and 2 tablespoons of the oil in a large bowl; season. Reserve 1 tablespoon of the oil mixture in a small bowl for serving; cover, refrigerate. Add lamb to large bowl; turn to coat. Cover; refrigerate for 1 hour or overnight.

2 Heat 1 tablespoon of the remaining oil in a small saucepan over low heat; add the thickly sliced green onion and cook, stirring occasionally, for 1 minute or until softened. Add vinegar and thyme; bring to a boil. Reduce heat; simmer, uncovered, for 5 minutes or until vinegar is reduced by half. Remove from heat; discard thyme. Stir in honey and currants; cool.

3 Separate Swiss chard leaves from stems. Chop stems coarsely; shred leaves coarsely. Heat remaining oil in a large deep frying pan over medium heat; cook chard stems for 3 minutes or until just softened. Add chard leaves; cook, stirring, for 3 minutes or until just wilted. Season to taste. Transfer to a platter; drizzle with vinegar mixture and sprinkle with pine nuts. Cover to keep warm.

4 Meanwhile, season lamb; cook lamb on a heated oiled grill pan (or on a grill under a broiler) over medium-high heat for 2 minutes each side for medium, or until cooked as desired.

5 Serve lamb drizzled with reserved oil mixture and Swiss chard topped with the thinly sliced green onion.

tips Wash Swiss chard well before using. You can use Tuscan kale instead of Swiss chard if you prefer.

make ahead Recipe can be prepared to the end of step 2 a day ahead. Keep vinegar mixture refrigerated.

kiwifruit & basil sherbet

PREP + COOK TIME

20 MINUTES (+ FREEZING)

SERVES 4

---

10 MEDIUM RIPE GREEN KIWIFRUIT,
PEELED, CHOPPED COARSELY, PLUS
4 GREEN KIWIFRUIT, PEELED, CHOPPED
COARSELY

1 TABLESPOON LIME JUICE

½ CUP LIGHT AGAVE SYRUP

⅓ CUP FIRMLY PACKED FRESH BASIL
LEAVES, CHOPPED COARSELY, PLUS 2
TABLESPOONS SMALL FRESH
BASIL LEAVES

⅓ CUP BUTTERMILK

1 Blend or process the 10 chopped kiwifruit, the juice, agave, basil, and buttermilk until smooth. Churn in an ice-cream maker according to manufacturer's instructions.

2 Spoon sherbet into a 4-cup loaf pan. Cover; freeze for 4 hours or overnight until firm.

3 Serve scoops of sherbet topped with 4 remaining chopped kiwifruit, and small basil leaves.

tip Freeze the loaf pan or container while the sherbet is churning so that it doesn't melt when transferred.

make ahead The sherbet can be made a week ahead.

serving suggestion Scoop the sherbet into glasses and top with iced green tea.

matcha mint slice

PREP + COOK TIME 35 MINUTES
(+ STANDING & FREEZING)
MAKES 25 SQUARES

YOU WILL NEED TO START THIS RECIPE A DAY AHEAD.

4 CUPS RAW CASHEWS

¾ CUP ALMOND MILK

1½ TABLESPOONS HONEY

1½ TABLESPOONS TAHINI

⅓ CUP COCONUT OIL, MELTED

1 TEASPOON VANILLA EXTRACT

1 TEASPOON PINK SEA SALT

1½ TEASPOONS MATCHA POWDER

1 TEASPOON PEPPERMINT ESSENCE, APPROXIMATELY

1 TEASPOON BLACK SESAME SEEDS

BASE

2 CUPS MEDJOOL DATES, PITTED

2 CUPS BUCKWHEAT GROATS

2 TABLESPOONS COCONUT OIL, MELTED

½ TEASPOON PINK SEA SALT

1 Place cashews in a large bowl with enough cold water to cover. Cover; stand overnight. Drain cashews. Rrinse under cold water; drain well.
2 Grease an 8 x 12–inch rectangular slice pan; line base and sides with parchment paper, extending the paper ¾-inch over the edge.
3 Make base.
4 Blend drained cashews, almond milk, honey, tahini, coconut oil, vanilla, and salt in a high-powered blender or food processor until smooth and creamy. Spread half the mixture over base in pan; freeze for 20 minutes or until firm.
5 Add matcha powder and peppermint essence to taste to the remaining cashew mixture; blend until well combined. Spoon matcha mixture over vanilla layer; smooth the surface, sprinkle with sesame seeds. Cover; freeze for at least 1 hour or until firm.
6 Cut slice into squares; place on plates. Stand at room temperature for 10 minutes to soften slightly before serving.
base Process dates using pulse button until coarsely chopped. Add buckwheat, coconut oil, and salt; pulse until just combined. Spread mixture evenly over base of pan. Freeze for at least 10 minutes while preparing filling.

tip Add a little extra matcha powder if the color is not strong enough.
make ahead Slice can be made up to 1 month ahead. Store in an airtight container in the freezer.

mini zucchini & lime loaves

PREP + COOK TIME 50 MINUTES
MAKES 8

¼ CUP WHOLE-WHEAT SELF-RISING FLOUR

½ CUP ALL-PURPOSE FLOUR

1 TEASPOON GROUND GINGER

½ TEASPOON BAKING SODA

½ TEASPOON SALT

¼ CUP PISTACHIOS, CHOPPED

¾ CUP COARSELY GRATED
ZUCCHINI (SEE TIP)

½ CUP COARSELY GRATED
RED APPLE (SEE TIP)

¾ CUP FIRMLY PACKED LIGHT BROWN
SUGAR

3 EGGS

⅔ CUP COCONUT OIL, MELTED

1 TEASPOON VANILLA EXTRACT

1 MEDIUM LIME

½ CUP GREEK-STYLE YOGURT

ZUCCHINI CHIPS

½ LARGE ZUCCHINI

¼ CUP HONEY

2 TEASPOONS FINELY GRATED LIME ZEST

1 TABLESPOON LIME JUICE

1 Preheat the oven to 300°F. Grease an 8-hole (⅔ cup) mini loaf pan; line base and long sides with parchment paper, extending the paper 1¼ inches over the edge.
2 Make zucchini chips.
3 Increase oven to 350°F. Sift flours, ginger, soda, and salt into a large bowl. Return husks to bowl; stir in pistachios.
4 Combine zucchini, apple, sugar, eggs, coconut oil, and vanilla in a large pitcher. Pour into flour mixture; stir until just combined. Spoon mixture into pan holes.
5 Bake loaves for 20 minutes or until a skewer inserted into the center comes out clean. Leave in pan for 5 minutes, before transferring to a wire rack. Brush with reserved honey syrup from zucchini chips; cool.
6 Top cooled cakes with zucchini chips. Remove zest from lime with a zester; sprinkle over cakes. Serve cakes with yogurt.
zucchini chips Line a baking sheet with parchment paper. Using a mandoline, thinly slice zucchini; pat dry with paper towels. Stir honey in a small saucepan over low heat until it comes to a simmer. Add zucchini; simmer, uncovered, for 3 minutes or until soft but still holding its shape. Drain zucchini over a pitcher or bowl; reserve syrup and cool slightly. Stir zest and juice into reserved syrup. Arrange zucchini, in a single layer, on the prepared baking sheet. Scrunch up slightly to make frilled edges. Bake for 15 minutes or until dry, removing outside slices when they are done to prevent over-browning. Cool.

tip You will need 1 medium zucchini and 1 medium apple for the grated quantities in the cake.
make ahead Cakes are best made on day of serving.

goat milk ricotta toasts with grapes & rosemary honey

PREP + COOK TIME
55 MINUTES (+ STANDING,
REFRIGERATION & COOLING)
SERVES 4

**YOU WILL NEED TO START THIS RECIPE
A DAY AHEAD.**

3 CUPS GOAT MILK

1 CUP POURING CREAM

½ TEASPOON SEA SALT FLAKES

¼ CUP LEMON JUICE

⅓ CUP HONEY

2 X 4-INCH SPRIGS FRESH ROSEMARY, PLUS
LEAVES FOR GARNISH

3 CUPS SEEDLESS GREEN GRAPES

2 TABLESPOONS VERJUICE

1-POUND LOAF SOURDOUGH BREAD, CUT
INTO EIGHT SLICES

1 Place goat milk, cream, and salt in a medium saucepan over medium heat; cook, stirring occasionally with a wooden spoon, for 15 minutes until it reaches 185°F on a kitchen thermometer, or just below boiling.
2 Remove pan from heat. Add juice; carefully swirl juice through mixture but do not stir. Let stand for 20 minutes or until the curds and whey have separated. Pour mixture into a muslin-lined large sieve over a deep bowl or pitcher. Cover; refrigerate for 24 hours or until thick.
3 Transfer ricotta to a large bowl; whisk until smooth. Season to taste. Place ricotta in an airtight container.
4 Meanwhile, combine honey and rosemary sprigs in a small saucepan. Bring just to a boil. Remove from heat; cool to room temperature.
5 Place grapes and verjuice in a large saucepan over high heat; coarsely mash grapes with a potato masher to extract the juice. Bring to a boil; simmer, uncovered, for 25 minutes or until thick and syrupy. Cool.
6 Meanwhile, place bread on a heated oiled grill pan (or grill) over high heat for 3 minutes each side or until grill marks appear.
7 Spread ricotta on toast, top with grape mixture. Serve drizzled with honey and garnished with rosemary leaves.

tips Leftover whey is great used instead of water in baking bread or pizza dough. Honey can be warmed in the microwave or until hot to infuse rosemary. The goat milk ricotta can be tossed through pasta in place of regular ricotta.
make ahead The ricotta can be made up to 3 days ahead; keep in an airtight container in the fridge.

cauliflower sushi with mushrooms & pickled daikon

**PREP + COOK TIME 50 MINUTES
(+ REFRIGERATION)
MAKES 4**

YOU WILL NEED TO START THIS RECIPE
8 HOURS AHEAD. YOU WILL NEED A
SUSHI MAT FOR THIS RECIPE.

2 POUNDS CAULIFLOWER,
CUT INTO FLORETS

2 TABLESPOONS COCONUT OIL

⅓ CUP SUSHI SEASONING

2½ OUNCES ENOKI MUSHROOMS

2½ OUNCES OYSTER MUSHROOMS

4 NORI SHEETS

¼ CUP SESAME SEEDS, TOASTED

1 SMALL BUNCH LONG CHIVES

⅓ CUP MAYONNAISE

2 TABLESPOONS TAMARI

1 TEASPOON WASABI PASTE,
APPROXIMATELY

PICKLED DAIKON

1 CUP SAKE

1 CUP RICE WINE VINEGAR

⅓ CUP LIGHT AGAVE SYRUP

2 TEASPOONS SEA SALT FLAKES

½ SMALL DAIKON, PEELED,
CUT INTO MATCHSTICKS

1 Make pickled daikon.

2 Preheat the oven to 400°F.

3 Process cauliflower in a food processor, in two batches, until it becomes fine crumbs. Heat coconut oil a large frying pan over medium-high heat; cook cauliflower, stirring, for 3 minutes or until cooked through; do not brown. Stir in sushi seasoning. Spread onto a large baking sheet; refrigerate for 20 minutes or until cool.

4 Meanwhile, trim ends from mushrooms and pull apart.

5 Place sushi mat on clean work surface. Place a nori sheet close to the bottom edge of the mat. Press a quarter of the cauliflower firmly onto nori, leaving a 2-inch border at the top. Make a slight furrow along the top and bottom of the cauliflower to help when rolling. Sprinkle 2 teaspoons of the seeds over cauliflower. Add a quarter of the enoki with the cap end facing outwards; place oyster mushrooms in a row next to enoki then 6 chives and a row of pickled daikon. Place a quarter of the mayonnaise next to the daikon.

6 To roll, fold over the bottom edge and press to roll up firmly. Wet fingers with cold water and dampen the nori border, then continue rolling to enclose. Roll sushi in mat between your hands a few times to make sure it's well formed. Transfer to a board. Brush top of roll lengthwise lighlty with a little water; sprinkle with remaining sesame seeds. Wipe mat clean and repeat with remaining cauliflower, sesame seeds, mushrooms, chives, daikon, and mayonnaise.

7 Cut each sushi roll into 5 pieces (don't be tempted to cut it thinner as this will squash the sushi—the cauliflower is not as firm as rice). Serve sushi with tamari and wasabi.

pickled daikon Combine sake, vinegar, agave syrup, and salt in a glass or ceramic bowl. Add daikon. Cover; refrigerate for 8 hours or overnight.

tips You can grate the cauliflower if you don't have a food processor. Keep a bowl of iced cold water to dip your hands in while making the sushi; this helps keep the sushi clean and stops the cauliflower sticking to your fingers. You can fill the sushi with your favorite filling ingredients.

make ahead Pickled daikon will keep in the pickling liquids for several weeks. Serve with ramen or in Asian-style salads and rice.

mushroom & barley "risotto"

PREP + COOK TIME 45 MINUTES
SERVES 4

1½ CUPS PEARL BARLEY

6 CUPS LOW-SODIUM CHICKEN STOCK

¼ CUP OLIVE OIL

7 SHALLOTS, SLICED THINLY

3 BAY LEAVES

3 CLOVES GARLIC, CRUSHED

⅓ POUND SHIITAKE MUSHROOMS, STALKS
REMOVED, QUARTERED

¼ POUND OYSTER MUSHROOMS, TORN

3 KING BROWN MUSHROOMS, QUARTERED
LENGTHWISE

1 CUP VERJUICE

¼ POUND ENOKI MUSHROOMS, TRIMMED,
SEPARATED

¼ CUP FINELY GRATED PARMESAN

¼ CUP CHOPPED FRESH CHIVES

1 Cook barley in a large saucepan of boiling water for 15 minutes; drain.
2 Bring stock to a boil in a medium saucepan. Reduce to a simmer; cover to keep warm.
3 Heat 2 tablespoons of the oil in a large heavy-based saucepan over medium heat; cook shallots and bay leaves, stirring, for 2 minutes or until soft. Add garlic; stirring, for a further 1 minute. Add shiitake, oyster, and king brown mushrooms; cook, stirring, for 5 minutes or until soft. Stir in barley and verjuice; cook, stirring, for 3 minutes or until verjuice is evaporated.
4 Stir in 2 cups of the simmering stock; cook, stirring, over low heat until liquid is absorbed. Continue adding stock, in 2-cup batches, stirring, until liquid is absorbed after each addition and barley is tender. Total cooking time should be about 20 minutes. Discard bay leaves.
5 Meanwhile, heat remaining oil a large frying pan over a high heat until beginning to smoke; cook enoki mushrooms, stirring, for 3 minutes or until golden.
6 Stir half the parmesan into barley mixture; season to taste. Serve in bowls topped with fried enoki, remaining parmesan, and the chives. Season with freshly ground black pepper. Serve immediately.

tips You can use risotto rice if you prefer; omit step 1 and reduce the stock to about 4 cups. Add the stock in ½-cup batches. Any mushroom medley can be used.
make ahead This recipe is best made close to serving.

miso, tofu & ginger broth

PREP + COOK TIME 25 MINUTES
SERVES 4

1 BUNCH CILANTRO

1 TABLESPOON OLIVE OIL

1 TABLESPOON FINELY GRATED
FRESH GINGER

1 MEDIUM LEEK, CHOPPED FINELY

2 CUPS VEGETABLE STOCK

¼ CUP DASHI MISO PASTE

4 CUPS WATER

1 SMALL DAIKON, PEELED, SLICED THINLY

1¼ POUNDS SILKEN TOFU, DRAINED, CUT
INTO ¾-INCH CUBES

¼ POUND BEAN SPROUTS, TRIMMED

⅓ POUND ENOKI MUSHROOMS, TRIMMED

1 FRESH LONG GREEN CHILE, SEEDS
REMOVED, CUT INTO LONG THIN STRIPS

1 TABLESPOON TOASTED SESAME SEEDS

1 TEASPOON CHILE OIL

1 Finely chop cilantro roots and stems; reserve leaves for serving.
2 Heat olive oil in a large saucepan over medium heat; cook chopped cilantro root and stems with ginger and leek, stirring, for 3 minutes or until leek is soft. Add stock, miso paste, and the water; bring to a boil. Add daikon; cook for 10 minutes or until daikon is just tender. Season to taste. Remove daikon with a slotted spoon to a small plate lined with paper towels.
3 Divide tofu, sprouts, and enoki between bowls. Ladle soup into bowls; top with daikon, fresh chile, sesame seeds, chile oil, and reserved cilantro leaves.

tip Dashi miso paste is available from Asian markets.
make ahead Soup is best made close to serving.

mushroom & black eye bean burgers

PREP + COOK TIME 30 MINUTES
(+ COOLING & REFRIGERATION)
SERVES 4

⅓ CUP OLIVE OIL

1 SMALL YELLOW ONION,
CHOPPED FINELY

½ POUND MUSHROOMS, QUARTERED

2 TABLESPOONS FRESH THYME LEAVES

1 CAN (15 OZ) BLACK EYE PEAS, DRAINED,
RINSED

1 EGG, BEATEN LIGHTLY

1 CUP FINELY GRATED PARMESAN

2 CLOVES GARLIC, CRUSHED

⅔ CUP BREAD CRUMBS

3 OUNCES CABBAGE, SLICED THINLY

2 TABLESPOONS LEMON JUICE

4 X SLIDER BUN, SPLIT

⅓ CUP MAYONNAISE

1 SMALL BULB FENNEL, SLICED THINLY,
FRONDS RESERVED

1 TABLESPOON HOT CHILE SAUCE

1 Heat 2 tablespoons of the oil in a large frying pan over medium heat; cook onion, mushrooms, and thyme, stirring occasionally, for 10 minutes or until softened and lightly golden. Cool 10 minutes.
2 Place mushroom mixture and beans in a food processor; pulse until chopped coarsely. Transfer mixture to a medium bowl; stir in egg, parmesan, garlic, and bread crumbs. Season to taste. Shape mixture into four patties; place on a plate. Cover; refrigerate for 30 minutes.
3 Heat remaining oil in same frying pan over medium heat; cook patties for 3 minutes each side, turning carefully, or until browned and heated through.
4 Meanwhile, combine cabbage and juice in a large bowl; season to taste.
5 Spread bun bases with mayonnaise; top with fennel, fennel fronds, patties, chile sauce, cabbage mixture, and bun tops.

tips Half button mushrooms and half cremini mushrooms were used to make this dish. For a stronger mushroom flavor, use cup or flat mushrooms instead of buttons. If the fennel doesn't have fronds, use dill, or just omit it.
make ahead Patties can be made a day ahead; keep covered in the fridge.

miso-roasted whole cauliflower

PREP + COOK TIME 45 MINUTES
SERVES 4 (OR 6 AS A SIDE)

2¾-POUND WHOLE CAULIFLOWER

1 CUP DRY SHERRY

¼ CUP WHITE (SHIRO) MISO PASTE

¼ CUP MAPLE SYRUP

2 TABLESPOONS OLIVE OIL

1 TABLESPOON FINELY GRATED
FRESH GINGER

2 CLOVES GARLIC, CRUSHED

2 TEASPOONS SESAME SEEDS

1 GREEN ONION, SLICED THINLY

1 Preheat the oven to 400°F.
2 Cut a cross in base of cauliflower with a sharp knife. Place cauliflower in a large, heavy-based cast iron casserole or deep ovenproof dish. Pour sherry into base of dish.
3 Combine miso, syrup, oil, ginger, and garlic in a small bowl; season. Spread over cauliflower. Cover dish with lid or foil; bake for 20 minutes. Sprinkle cauliflower with sesame seeds; bake, uncovered, for a further 15 minutes or until cauliflower is tender and browned lightly.
4 Serve cauliflower topped with green onion.

tips If you don't have space in your oven to cook a whole cauliflower, cut it into six wedges and lay them flat in a baking dish; bake them, uncovered, for the second amount of cooking time. You can also roast six baby cauliflowers for individual serves.
serving suggestion Serve this as part of a roast dinner or as a main for vegetarians.

mushroom & goat cheese ravioli with tarragon brown butter

PREP + COOK TIME 40 MINUTES
(+ STANDING & COOLING)
SERVES 4

½ OUNCE DRIED PORCINI MUSHROOMS

½ CUP BOILING WATER

1 TABLESPOON OLIVE OIL

½ POUND CREMINI MUSHROOMS, CHOPPED FINELY

1 CLOVE GARLIC, CRUSHED

3 OUNCES GOAT CHEESE, CRUMBLED

1 TABLESPOON FINELY CHOPPED FRESH TARRAGON LEAVES

24 GOW GEE WRAPPERS

⅓ CUP GRATED PARMESAN

1 TABLESPOON FRESH CHERVIL LEAVES

TARRAGON BROWN BUTTER

5 TABLESPOONS BUTTER, CHOPPED

¼ CUP WALNUTS, CHOPPED

1 TABLESPOON TARRAGON LEAVES

1 Place porcini in a heatproof bowl with the boiling water; let stand for 15 minutes or until soft. Drain, reserving ¼ cup of the soaking liquid. Finely chop mushrooms.

2 Heat oil in a medium frying pan over medium-high heat; cook cremini mushrooms, stirring, for 4 minutes or until soft. Add garlic; cook, stirring, for 1 minute or until fragrant. Stir in porcini and reserved soaking liquid; cook, stirring, for 5 minutes or until excess liquid is evaporated but mushrooms are still moist. Season to taste. Transfer mixture to a heatproof bowl; cool to room temperature. Reserve frying pan, without rinsing, for tarragon brown butter.

3 Add goat cheese and tarragon to cooled mushroom mixture; mix well.

4 Place 12 gow gee wrappers on a clean work surface. Divide the mushroom mixture between wrappers. Dampen edges of wrappers with a little water; top with remaining wrappers, pressing edges to seal.

5 Cook ravioli in a large saucepan of boiling salted water, in batches, for 2 minutes or until they float to the surface. Remove ravioli with a slotted spoon; place in a single layer on a baking sheet. Cover to keep warm.

6 Meanwhile, make tarragon brown butter.

7 Serve ravioli topped with tarragon brown butter, parmesan, and chervil. Season with freshly ground black pepper.

tarragon brown butter Melt butter in reserved frying pan; add walnuts and tarragon. Heat gently until butter begins to turn a nutty brown color. Transfer immediately to a small heatproof bowl or pitcher.

make ahead The filling can be made a day ahead.

chicken, quinoa & endive salad

PREP + COOK TIME
30 MINUTES (+ STANDING)
SERVES 4

⅓ CUP WHITE QUINOA

3 CUPS WATER

2 CUPS CHICKEN STOCK

¾ POUND CHICKEN BREAST FILLETS

⅓ CUP APPLE CIDER VINEGAR

2½ TABLESPOONS HONEY

¼ CUP OLIVE OIL

⅓ POUND BRUSSELS SPROUTS, TRIMMED, SHREDDED FINELY

2 BELGIAN ENDIVE, LEAVES SEPARATED

1 SMALL GRANNY SMITH APPLE, SLICED THINLY

½ CUP TOASTED HAZELNUTS, SKINS REMOVED, CHOPPED COARSELY

1 Bring quinoa and 1 cup water to a boil in a small saucepan; cook, covered, over low heat for 10 minutes or until tender. Drain well; cool.
2 Meanwhile, bring stock and the remaining 2 cups water to a boil in a medium saucepan. Add chicken; return to boil. Reduce heat; simmer, covered, for 5 minutes. Remove pan from heat; stand chicken in poaching liquid for 15 minutes or until cooked through. Remove chicken from pan (reserve poaching liquid for another use, see **tips**); shred chicken coarsely. You will need 2 cups.
3 Place vinegar, honey, and oil in a screw-top jar; shake well. Season to taste.
4 Place sprouts, endive, apple, and chicken in a large bowl with dressing; toss gently to combine. Serve salad topped with hazelnuts.

tips Use a mandoline or V-slicer to cut the brussels sprouts and apple. The unused chicken poaching liquid can be kept in the fridge for up to 3 days or frozen for up to 6 months. Use it in soups, casseroles, or sauces.

grilled haloumi, white nectarine & kohlrabi salad

PREP + COOK TIME 15 MINUTES
SERVES 4

8 OUNCES HALOUMI

1 TABLESPOON OLIVE OIL

2 BELGIAN ENDIVE, TRIMMED

1 WHITE KOHLRABI, PEELED, TRIMMED, CUT INTO MATCHSTICKS

2 TEASPOONS HONEY

4 RIPE WHITE NECTARINES OR PEACHES, HALVED, PITS REMOVED, SLICED

2 TABLESPOONS ALMOND DUKKAH

HONEY & LEMON DRESSING

½ CUP EXTRA-VIRGIN OLIVE OIL

1 TEASPOON FINELY GRATED LEMON ZEST

2 TABLESPOONS LEMON JUICE

2 TEASPOONS HONEY

1 TEASPOON FRESH ROSEMARY LEAVES

1 SMALL CLOVE GARLIC, CRUSHED

1 Drain haloumi; pat dry with paper towels. Cut lengthwise into eight slices. Toss in oil; season with freshly ground black pepper.
2 Make honey and lemon dressing.
3 Separate outer endive leaves; halve small centers. Place endive in a large bowl with kohlrabi and half the dressing; toss gently to combine.
4 Cook haloumi, in batches, on a heated grill pan (or grill or frying pan) over high heat for 1 minute each side or until golden. Drizzle with honey; cook for a further 15 seconds or until beginning to color. Remove from heat; thinly slice half the haloumi.
5 Layer haloumi, endive mixture, and nectarine slices on a large platter. Drizzle with remaining dressing and sprinkle with dukkah.
honey & lemon dressing Place ingredients in a screw-top jar; shake well. Season.

tips If nectarines or peaches are out of season, use Asian pears or champagne melon. If you are using slightly under-ripe nectarines, peaches, or pears, brush them with a little oil and honey then grill for 1 minute to help soften the flesh and release their flavor.

crisp fish parcels with lychee & coconut salad

PREP + COOK TIME 50 MINUTES
SERVES 4

- 1 SMALL COCONUT
- 4 SKINLESS WHITE FISH FILLETS (ABOUT ⅓ POUND EACH), BONES REMOVED
- 4-INCH STALK FRESH LEMONGRASS, CHOPPED VERY FINELY
- ½ CUP LOOSELY PACKED FRESH CILANTRO LEAVES
- 4 X 8½-INCH RICE-PAPER ROUNDS
- 2 TABLESPOONS VEGETABLE OIL
- 1 LARGE LEBANESE CUCUMBER, PEELED
- 1 POUND CANNED LYCHEES IN SYRUP
- 1 MEDIUM SHALLOT, SLICED THINLY
- 1 TABLESPOON LIME JUICE
- 2 TEASPOONS HOISIN SAUCE
- 1 MEDIUM LIME, CUT INTO WEDGES

1 Preheat the oven to 350°F.

2 Place coconut in a shallow-sided baking pan or dish to catch the coconut water. Firmly crack open coconut around the center with the blunt edge of a cleaver; drain out the water. Place coconut on a baking sheet; roast for 10 minutes to loosen the flesh. Pull flesh away from shell. Use a vegetable peeler to shave half the coconut into thin slices. Place coconut slices and 2 tablespoons of the reserved strained coconut water in a large bowl; toss well. Reserve remaining coconut for another use (see tips).

3 Pat fish dry with paper towels. Top each fillet with lemongrass and cilantro. Working with one at a time, place a rice paper round in a medium bowl of warm water until just softened. Lift rice paper from water; place on a clean surface. Place one fish fillet in the center of rice paper, cilantro-side down. Fold over two short ends; roll to enclose filling. Repeat with remaining rice paper rounds and fish fillets.

4 Heat oil in a large frying pan over medium-high heat; cook fish parcels for 6 minutes or until browned lightly on both sides and cooked through.

5 Meanwhile, using a vegetable peeler, peel cucumber into long thin ribbons. Drain lychees over a pitcher or bowl; reserve ¼ cup syrup. Cut lychees in half. Add lychees, cucumber, and shallot to sliced coconut in large bowl. In a small bowl, whisk lime juice, hoisin sauce, and reserved lychee syrup until combined. Drizzle dressing over salad.

6 Serve fish parcels with salad and lime wedges.

tips You can use any fresh white fish fillet you prefer. This recipe won't work as well with frozen and thawed fish as it releases extra liquid during cooking and will make the rice paper soggy. Remaining coconut can be refrigerated in an airtight container for 3 days.

salt-crusted whole fish with celeriac remoulade

PREP + COOK TIME
45 MINUTES (+ STANDING)
SERVES 4

2 POUNDS WHOLE SNAPPER, CLEANED

1 MEDIUM LEMON, SLICED

2 FRESH DILL SPRIGS, PLUS ⅓ CUP LOOSELY PACKED FRESH DILL SPRIGS

5 CUPS COARSE COOKING SALT

3 EGG WHITES

⅓ CUP LOOSELY PACKED FRESH FLAT-LEAF PARSLEY LEAVES

CELERY ROOT REMOULADE

1 SMALL CELERY ROOT

⅓ CUP MAYONNAISE

2 TABLESPOONS THINLY SLICED CORNICHONS

1 TABLESPOON LEMON JUICE

1 TABLESPOON DIJON MUSTARD

1 TABLESPOON SALTED BABY CAPERS, RINSED

1 Preheat the oven to 400°F. Line a large baking sheet with foil.
2 Use kitchen scissors to snip off fish fins and trim the tail. Place lemon slices and dill sprigs in fish cavity.
3 Combine salt and egg whites in a large bowl until the consistency feels like sand. Spread one-third of the salt mixture on the prepared baking sheet. Place fish on top of salt then cover fish completely with remaining salt mixture, molding it tightly around the fish to seal.
4 Bake fish for 25 minutes. To check if the fish is cooked, insert a sharp knife through the crust into the thickest part of the fish; wait 5 seconds. Slowly withdraw knife and touch the flat side of the blade to the inside of your wrist. If the blade is hot, the fish is cooked. Let stand for 10 minutes.
5 Meanwhile, make celery root remoulade.
6 Break crust around edges of fish and gently lift the crust off. Remove and discard fish skin. Serve fish with remoulade, parsley, and remaining dill sprigs.
celery root remoulade Peel celery root; cut into matchsticks. Place celery root in a medium heatproof bowl with enough boiling water to cover; let stand for 30 seconds, drain. Refresh in another bowl of iced water; drain. Return celery root to bowl with remaining ingredients; mix well. Season to taste.

tips The salt crust keeps the fish moist and lightly seasons the flesh during cooking. To fillet the fish for serving, make a diagonal cut near the gills and tails, then down the middle of the back along the spine. Lift the top fillet off with a spatula. Peel away the bones and remove base fillet. Remove any salt mixture clinging to the fish.
make ahead Celery root remoulade can be made a day ahead. Keep, covered, in the fridge.

cabbage & Asian pear slaw with pork

PREP + COOK TIME 30 MINUTES
(+ REFRIGERATION & STANDING)
SERVES 4

1 TABLESPOON TAMARI

1 TABLESPOON SESAME OIL

1 TEASPOON FIVE-SPICE POWDER

1 TEASPOON FINELY GRATED LEMON ZEST

1¼ POUNDS PORK FILLET

2 TABLESPOONS MAPLE SYRUP

1 MEDIUM JICAMA, PEELED,
CUT INTO MATCHSTICKS

½ POUND NAPA CABBAGE, TORN

1 MEDIUM ASIAN PEAR, SLICED THINLY

¼ CUP LOOSELY PACKED FRESH CILANTRO
LEAVES

⅓ CUP LEMON JUICE

⅓ CUP EXTRA-VIRGIN OLIVE OIL

2 TABLESPOONS SESAME SEEDS, TOASTED

1 Preheat the oven to 400°F. Line a medium baking sheet with parchment paper.
2 Combine tamari, sesame oil, five-spice, and zest in a large bowl. Trim pork of any fat. Add pork to bowl, turn to coat; season. Cover; refrigerate for 30 minutes.
3 Transfer pork to the prepared baking sheet. Roast for 20 minutes or until just cooked through. Transfer pork to a plate; drizzle with half the syrup. Cover loosely with foil; let stand for 10 minutes.
4 Meanwhile, combine jicama, cabbage, and pear in a large bowl. Add combined juice, olive oil, sesame seeds, and remaining maple syrup; toss gently to combine. Season.
5 Slice pork; serve with slaw and cilantro.

tip Jicama, pronounced *hi-kah-ma*, is also known as a yam bean. It's mostly served raw in salads and salsas. Keep it at room temperature or refrigerate once cut. It must be peeled before use.

sesame fish lettuce cups

PREP + COOK TIME 40 MINUTES
SERVES 4

1 SMALL YELLOW ONION, PEELED, SLICED THINLY

⅓ CUP WHITE BALSAMIC VINEGAR

3 GEM LETTUCE (ABOUT 1 POUND TOTAL), TRIMMED, LEAVES SEPARATED (SEE TIPS)

½ POUND RED RADISHES, TRIMMED, SLICED THINLY

1 BABY FENNEL BULB, TRIMMED, SLICED THINLY LENGTHWISE

2 TABLESPOONS LEMON JUICE

1½ POUNDS BONELESS WHITE FISH FILLETS

⅔ CUP SESAME SEEDS

⅓ CUP OLIVE OIL

½ CUP LOOSELY PACKED FRESH WATERCRESS

6½ OUNCES TZATZIKI

1 Place onion in a small heatproof glass or ceramic dish. Bring vinegar to a boil in a small saucepan over medium heat; pour over onion, stir well. Cool.
2 Meanwhile, place lettuce leaves in a large bowl of iced water. Place radish in a medium bowl of iced water. Stand 5 minutes; drain. Dry lettuce and radish with paper towels.
3 Combine fennel and juice in a medium bowl.
4 Cut fish into 16 x ¾-inch wide strips. Coat fish in sesame seeds; season. Heat half the oil in a large frying pan over medium heat; cook half the fish for 5 minutes or until browned all over and just cooked through. Drain on paper towel; cover to keep warm. Repeat with remaining oil and fish.
5 Place 16 large lettuce cups on a serving platter; reserve remaining for another use. Top with watercress, fish, tzatziki, fennel, drained pickled onions, and radishes.

tips You can use romaine or other crisp lettuce leaves instead of gem lettuce, if you like. If you prefer, combine Greek-style yogurt with chopped fresh mint instead of the tzatziki.
serving suggestions Serve as a light lunch or dinner, or with a Greek salad for a more substantial meal.

creamy chicken pies with celery root & parsnip mash

PREP + COOK TIME 50 MINUTES

SERVES 6

⅓ CUP PLUS 1 TABLESPOON BUTTER

2 MEDIUM LEEKS, WHITE PART SLICED THINLY

4 CLOVES GARLIC, CRUSHED

1 CUP WHITE WINE

⅓ CUP ALL-PURPOSE FLOUR

2 CUPS CHICKEN STOCK

3¼ CUPS MILK

⅓ POUND BABY SPINACH LEAVES

1 TABLESPOON CHOPPED FRESH TARRAGON LEAVES

1½ POUNDS CHICKEN BREAST FILLETS, CUT INTO ¾-INCH PIECES

2 MEDIUM CELERY ROOT, PEELED, CUT INTO ¾-INCH PIECES

2 LARGE PARSNIPS, PEELED, CUT INTO ¾-INCH PIECES

1 TABLESPOON DIJON MUSTARD

1 CUP FINELY GRATED PARMESAN

1 Preheat the oven to 400°F. Grease three 2-cup ovenproof dishes

2 Melt ½ cup of the butter in a large saucepan over medium heat; cook leek and garlic, stirring, for 8 minutes or until leek is soft. Add wine; simmer, uncovered, for 3 minutes or until most of the liquid is evaporated.

3 Add flour; cook, stirring, for 2 minutes or until mixture bubbles and thickens. Gradually stir in combined stock and 2 cups of the milk; cook, stirring, until sauce boils and thickens. Stir in spinach and tarragon; season to taste. Stir in chicken; remove from heat. Spoon mixture into dishes.

4 Meanwhile, boil, steam or microwave celery root and parsnip until tender; drain. Return to pan; mash vegetables until smooth. Stir in remaining butter, remaining milk, and the mustard. Season to taste.

5 Spoon mash over chicken mixture in dishes; make peaks in the surface with a spoon or fork. Sprinkle with parmesan.

6 Bake pies for 20 minutes or until mash is browned lightly and chicken is cooked through.

tips For a gluten-free version, swap plain flour for gluten-free plain flour. You can use any combination of root vegetables for the mash topping including potatoes, orange sweet potato, white sweet potato, and turnip. The flavor of this sauce relies on gentle slow cooking of the leek and garlic to release natural sweetness. You can also bake one large pie in a 2-quart rectangular ovenproof dish.

Cauliflower provides nourishment across a wide group of nutritional categories to reduce your risk of cardiovascular disease and cancer.

This is down to the arsenal of vitamins and a group of important antioxidants called flavonoids, and the sulphur-containing compounds they contain, which act as cancer-fighting agents. Other nutrients help protect the body against free-radical damage. Cauliflower is also a good source of vitamins C, A, and E, and folate and potassium.

Caulislaw

Thinly shave ½ small cauliflower and 1 green apple. Finely chop 2 green onions. Combine cauliflower, apple, onion and a handful of toasted crumbled walnuts and torn mint leaves in a bowl. Drizzle with an olive oil and lemon dressing. Add in pieces of torn buffalo mozzarella, if you like.

When cauliflower is eaten raw, the uptake of antioxidants into the blood stream is improved.

CAULI STEAKS & GRAVY

Place a whole cauliflower stem-side down, cut in half through the middle, then cut each half in the same direction for four steaks. Brush with oil, garlic, and little ground turmeric and coriander. Fry in batches, 3 minutes each side or until golden. Finish in a 350°F oven with a couple of stalks of rosemary, for 12 minutes or until tender. Fry ¼ lb each oyster and cremini mushrooms, in a little oil and butter over high heat until crisp; remove from pan. Add a little more oil to pan; cook 1 finely chopped shallot and 1 clove crushed garlic until soft. Add 2 tablespoons dry white wine, cook until almost evaporated, add mushrooms and 1½ cups vegetable stock, reduce by half. Blend 2 teaspoons cornstarch with 1 tablespoon cold water; stir into gravy until mixture boils and thickens.

The best cooking methods

It seems we've been doing it wrong all these years. Traditional boiled cauli, the sure-fire step toward soggy disappointment, has been usurped. Steaming briefly will preserve nutrients better, but it's roasting, chargrilling, pan-frying, and stir-frying it as rice that have been whipping cooks into a taste frenzy. It seems these dry, and often high-heat cooking methods, amplify its natural caramel sweetness. As well as eating it cooked, there are benefits to consuming it raw, such as more intact plant cells reaching the colon, which is considered beneficial in reducing the risk of colon cancer.

almond-crusted chicken schnitzel with fennel & Asian pear salad

PREP + COOK TIME
45 MINUTES (+ REFRIGERATION)
SERVES 4

2 LARGE CHICKEN BREAST FILLETS, HALVED
HORIZONTALLY

2 EGGS

2 TEASPOONS WATER

1 CUP GROUND ALMONDS

1 CLOVE GARLIC, CRUSHED

1 TEASPOON FINELY GRATED LEMON ZEST

¼ CUP COARSELY CHOPPED
FRESH FLAT-LEAF PARSLEY

⅓ CUP OLIVE OIL

FENNEL & ASIAN PEAR SALAD

2 TABLESPOONS OLIVE OIL

1 TABLESPOON LEMON JUICE

1 FENNEL BULB, QUARTERED

1 ASIAN PEAR, SLICED THINLY

4 RED RADISHES, TRIMMED,
CUT INTO THIN WEDGES

4 CUPS CHOPPED ICEBERG LETTUCE

½ CUP SHAVED PARMESAN

1 Pound chicken between two sheets of plastic wrap or parchment paper with a rolling pin or meat mallet until ½-inch thick.

2 Lightly beat egg and the water in a shallow dish. Combine ground almonds, garlic, zest, and parsley in a shallow dish; season. Dip chicken, one piece at a time, in egg; dip in almond mixture to coat, pressing firmly. Place on a plate, refrigerate for 30 minutes.

3 Meanwhile, make fennel and Asian pear salad.

4 Heat oil in a large frying pan over medium-high heat; cook schnitzels for 2 minutes on each side or until just cooked through. Drain on paper towels.

5 Serve schnitzels with salad.

fennel & Asian pear salad Place oil and juice in screw-top jar; season, shake well to combine. Reserve fronds from fennel. Using a mandoline or V-slicer, shave fennel. Place shaved fennel in a medium bowl with pear, radishes, and lettuce; toss gently to combine. Just before serving, add dressing, parmesan and reserved fennel fronds; toss to combine.

tips If Asian pears are not in season, this salad also tastes great with apples instead. Fennel fronds can be kept in a bag in the fridge; use in place of dill in salads, sprinkle over cooked pork or fish, or chop and stir into casseroles.

squid skewers with celery, fennel & daikon

PREP + COOK TIME

35 MINUTES (+ REFRIGERATION)

SERVES 4

YOU NEED 12 SMALL BAMBOO SKEWERS.
SOAK THEM IN COLD WATER FOR AT LEAST
30 MINUTES BEFORE USING.

10 SMALL CLEANED SQUID HOODS
(SEE TIP)

2 CLOVES GARLIC, CHOPPED FINELY

½ TEASPOON GROUND WHITE PEPPER

1 TABLESPOON FINELY GRATED
FRESH GINGER

¼ CUP OLIVE OIL

½ CUP LEMON JUICE

1 FENNEL BULB, TRIMMED, SLICED THINLY

1 DAIKON, PEELED, CUT INTO MATCHSTICKS

2 CELERY STICKS, LEAVES RESERVED,
SLICED THINLY

2 TABLESPOONS FRESH FLAT-LEAF
PARSLEY LEAVES

¼ CUP LOOSELY PACKED FRESH
MINT LEAVES

3 TABLESPOONS UNSALTED BUTTER,
CHOPPED

1 TABLESPOON SESAME SEEDS, TOASTED

1 Cut squid hoods in half lengthwise. Using a sharp knife, score inside surface in a crisscross pattern at ¼-inch intervals. Cut into 1½-inch strips. Thread loosely onto 12 small bamboo skewers.

2 Combine garlic, pepper, ginger, oil, and half the juice in a shallow dish. Add squid skewers; turn to coat. Cover; refrigerate for 1 hour.

3 Combine fennel, daikon, celery, reserved celery leaves, parsley, and mint in a large bowl; season. Arrange on a platter.

4 Drain squid; reserve marinade. Place marinade in a small saucepan; simmer over low heat for 4 minutes or until reduced slightly.

5 Cook squid on a heated oiled grill pan (or grill) over high heat for 2 minutes each side or until golden brown. Transfer to salad.

6 Stir butter and remaining juice into marinade; season to taste. Drizzle sauce over squid; sprinkle with sesame seeds.

tip Often cleaned squid hoods are large and thick. You can buy 2 pounds of whole small calamari and clean the squid yourself. To do this, gently pull head and tentacles with internal sac away from body. Remove clear cartilage (quill) from inside body. Remove and discard side fins and skin from body with salted fingers. Wash body; pat dry.

roasted rosemary pork, fennel & potatoes

PREP + COOK TIME
1 HOUR 15 MINUTES (+ STANDING)
SERVES 4

1 TABLESPOON FINELY CHOPPED FRESH ROSEMARY LEAVES

2 TEASPOONS FENNEL SEEDS

½ TEASPOON RED PEPPER FLAKES

¼ CUP OLIVE OIL

4 SMALL FENNEL BULBS, HALVED

1½ POUNDS FINGERLING POTATOES, HALVED LENGTHWISE

1 POUND PORK FILLET

1 MEDIUM LEMON, CUT INTO WEDGES

1 Preheat the oven to 425°F.
2 Combine rosemary, seeds, pepper flakes, and oil in a small bowl; season. Place fennel and potato in a large baking dish. Drizzle with two-thirds of the rosemary mixture; toss to combine. Roast for 30 minutes.
3 Rub pork with remaining rosemary mixture. Stir potato and fennel; place pork on top of vegetables. Roast for 25 minutes or until pork is just cooked through. Cover loosely with foil; stand in a warm place for 5 minutes.
4 Slice pork. Serve with potato, fennel, and lemon wedges.

tip You could replace the pork with chicken breasts on the bone.

cauliflower hummus with spiced lamb

PREP + COOK TIME
50 MINUTES (+ STANDING)
SERVES 4 AS A STARTER

½ CAULIFLOWER, CUT INTO FLORETS

3 CLOVES GARLIC, UNPEELED

⅓ CUP OLIVE OIL

1 SMALL WHITE ONION,
CHOPPED FINELY

½ POUND GROUND LAMB

1 TEASPOON POMEGRANATE MOLASSES

1 TABLESPOON TAHINI

2½ TABLESPOONS LEMON JUICE

⅓ CUP GREEK-STYLE YOGURT

½ TEASPOON SEA SALT

1 TABLESPOON COLD WATER

6 GREEK-STYLE GYROS WRAPS

1½ TEASPOONS DUKKAH

½ TEASPOON FINELY GRATED LEMON ZEST

1 MEDIUM LEMON, CUT INTO WEDGES

1 Preheat the oven to 400°F. Line two baking sheets with parchment paper.
2 Using a mandoline or V-slicer, thinly slice 1½ ounces of the cauliflower; reserve for serving. Combine remaining cauliflower and garlic with 2 teaspoons of the oil in a large bowl; season, transfer to prepared baking sheets. Roast for 20 minutes or until cauliflower is tender. Let stand for 15 minutes or until almost cool. Squeeze garlic from skin.
3 Meanwhile, heat another 2 teaspoons of the oil in a large frying pan over medium heat. Cook onion, stirring, for 2 minutes or until softened. Add lamb; cook, stirring, for 8 minutes or until lamb is browned and slightly crisp. Stir in molasses; season to taste. Cover to keep warm.
4 Blend or process roasted cauliflower and garlic with tahini, juice, yogurt, salt, and the water until well combined.
5 Working in batches, brush wraps with 2 tablespoons of the remaining oil; bake for 1 minute each side or until lightly golden. Cut into strips or wedges. Cover to keep warm.
6 Spread cauliflower hummus on a platter; top with lamb mixture and reserved cauliflower. Drizzle with remaining oil, sprinkle with dukkah and zest. Serve hummus with wraps and lemon wedges.

make ahead The lamb mixture can be made a day ahead; reheat before serving. The hummus is best made on the day of serving. If making ahead, leave out the yogurt; reheat the hummus until just warm then stir in the yogurt before serving.

coconut Tapioca puddings

PREP + COOK TIME 30 MINUTES
(+ STANDING & REFRIGERATION)
SERVES 4

1 CUP SEED TAPIOCA

1⅔ CANNED COCONUT MILK

1 CUP WATER

⅓ CUP SUPERFINE SUGAR

1 TEASPOON FINELY GRATED LIME ZEST

1 TEASPOON VANILLA EXTRACT

**8 FRESH LYCHEES, PEELED,
SEEDS REMOVED, TORN**

**½ CUP THINLY SLICED YOUNG
COCONUT FLESH**

1 MEDIUM LIME

4 WHITE EDIBLE FLOWERS, OPTIONAL

1 Place tapioca in a large bowl with enough cold water to cover. Let stand for 2 hours. Drain. Rinse well; drain.
2 Meanwhile, stir coconut milk, the water, sugar, zest, and vanilla in a medium saucepan until sugar is dissovled. Bring to a simmer; simmer, uncovered, for 5 minutes. Cool. Refrigerate until cold.
3 Add tapioca to a medium saucepan of boiling water; simmer, uncovered, for 10 minutes or until tapioca is clear. Drain well. Stir tapioca into coconut milk mixture.
4 Divide tapioca mixture into bowls or glasses; top with lychees and coconut flesh. Finely grate zest from the lime, sprinkle on puddings; top with flowers.

tip Seed tapioca is a starch extract, made from the tubers of the cassava plant. You can substitute with sago, a similar product from sago palms.
make ahead Puddings can be made a day ahead; keep refrigerated.

milk pudding with honeydew melon granita

PREP + COOK TIME
40 MINUTES (+ COOLING,
FREEZING & REFRIGERATION)
SERVES 4

⅔ CUP AGAVE SYRUP

½ TEASPOON FINELY GRATED
FRESH GINGER

3 CARDAMOM PODS, BRUISED

1 CUP WATER

1½ POUNDS HONEYDEW MELON, PEELED,
CHOPPED COARSELY, PLUS 3 OUNCES
HONEYDEW MELON, PEELED THINLY

1 TEASPOON FINELY GRATED LIME ZEST

MILK PUDDING

¼ CUP CORNSTARCH

2½ CUPS MILK

¼ CUP SUPERFINE SUGAR

1 TEASPOON ROSE WATER

1 Place agave syrup, ginger, cardamom, and the water in a small saucepan; bring to a boil. Reduce heat to low; simmer, uncovered, for 10 minutes or until thickened slightly. Remove from heat; cool.

2 Blend or process the coarsely chopped melon until smooth. Add strained syrup mixture; process until combined. Pour into a wide shallow pan or baking sheet; freeze for 1 hour. Using a fork, scrape ice from edges back into liquid. Return to freezer or until beginning to freeze. Repeat another three times until granita looks like crushed ice. Freeze until ready to serve.

3 Meanwhile, make milk pudding.

4 Flake granita with a fork; serve puddings topped with granita, thinly peeled melon, and the lime zest.

milk pudding Combine cornstarch and ½ cup of the milk in a small bowl until smooth. Place remaining milk and sugar in a medium saucepan over medium heat; stir until sugar dissolves. Whisk in cornstarch mixture; cook, stirring constantly, until mixture bubbles and thickens. Remove from heat; stir in rose water. Pour mixture into four 1-cup serving bowls or glasses; cool. Cover with plastic wrap; refrigerate for 2 hours or until cold.

tip Use maize cornstarch for a gluten-free dessert.
make ahead Recipe can be made a day ahead.

banana, coconut & rosemary nice-cream

PREP + COOK TIME
20 MINUTES (+ OVERNIGHT
FREEZING & STANDING)
SERVES 4

**YOU WILL NEED TO START THIS RECIPE
A DAY AHEAD.**

10 RIPE BANANAS, CUT INTO ½-INCH SLICES

1½ CUPS CANNED COCONUT MILK

6 SMALL SPRIGS FRESH ROSEMARY

2 TABLESPOONS HONEY

⅓ CUP TOASTED FLAKED COCONUT

1 Line 2 large baking sheets with parchment paper. Place banana slices on the prepared baking sheets and cover; freeze overnight or until firm.
2 Stir coconut milk, 2 rosemary sprigs, and honey in a small saucepan over medium-low heat; bring to a simmer. Simmer gently for 5 minutes. Remove pan from heat; cover, let stand for at least 20 minutes. Remove rosemary sprigs; discard 1 sprig. Pick leaves from remaining sprig; reserve.
3 Blend banana in a high-powered blender until very finely chopped. Add ⅔ cup of the coconut milk mixture and reserved rosemary leaves. Blend until mixture forms a soft serve ice-cream texture, scraping down the sides if required.
4 Spoon banana mixture into glasses or bowls; drizzle with remaining coconut milk mixture. Top with coconut flakes and 4 remaining rosemary sprigs.

tip Bananas should be ripe for the best flavor and texture.
make ahead The texture of the nice-cream is best as soon as it is made, but it can be frozen for up to 2 days ahead.

grilled watermelon & mozzarella salad with raspberry dressing

PREP + COOK TIME 15 MINUTES
(+ REFRIGERATION)
SERVES 4 AS A STARTER OR SIDE

¼ WATERMELON

3 CUPS LOOSELY PACKED WATERCRESS

2 BALLS BUFFALO MOZZARELLA, TORN

1 TABLESPOON FINELY GRATED
LEMON ZEST

1 TABLESPOON DRIED PINK PEPPERCORNS

RASPBERRY DRESSING

¼ POUND FRESH RASPBERRIES

2 TABLESPOONS RASPBERRY VINEGAR

1 TABLESPOON HONEY

2 TABLESPOONS OLIVE OIL

1 Make raspberry dressing.
2 Remove rind from watermelon. Cut wedge in half lengthwise then into ½-inch thick triangles.
3 Heat a large grill pan (or a grill or broiler) until smoking hot. Grill watermelon, in batches, for 50 seconds each side or until charred lightly. Transfer to a plate; refrigerate for 20 minutes.
4 Arrange watermelon and watercress on a platter. Top with mozzarella, zest, and peppercorns; drizzle with dressing.
raspberry dressing Place half the raspberries in a medium bowl; mash lightly with a fork. Stir in vinegar, honey, and oil; season to taste. Tear remaining raspberries in half, stir into dressing.

tips Grill any ripe seasonal melon for this dish. You can use bocconcini instead of mozzarella. You can use arugula or mixed salad leaves instead of watercress.
serving suggestions Serve with grilled meat or fish.

Tomato & strawberry gazpacho

PREP TIME 15 MINUTES
(+ REFRIGERATION)
SERVES 4

- -

6 SMALL TOMATOES

- -

½ POUND STRAWBERRIES

- -

**½ SMALL RED ONION,
CHOPPED COARSELY**

- -

1 RED BELL PEPPER, CHOPPED COARSELY

- -

**1 LEBANESE CUCUMBER, PEELED, CHOPPED
COARSELY**

- -

¼ CUP SHERRY VINEGAR

- -

1 FRESH LONG RED CHILE, CHOPPED

- -

1 CLOVE GARLIC, CRUSHED

- -

**½ CUP LOOSELY PACKED FRESH
BASIL LEAVES, PLUS 2 TABLESPOONS SMALL
FRESH BASIL LEAVES**

- -

¼ CUP PLUS 2 TEASPOONS OLIVE OIL

- -

1 CUP WATER

- -

1½ OUNCES GOAT CHEESE, CRUMBLED

- -

- -

1 Coarsely chop 5 tomatoes and 6½ ounces of the strawberries. Place in a large, nonreactive bowl with onion, bell pepper, cucumber, vinegar, chile, garlic, the ½ cup loosely packed basil, the ½ cup oil, and the water; season to taste. Cover; refrigerate for 3 hours.

2 Blend or process tomato mixture until smooth; season. Pour into serving glasses.

3 Finely chop remaining tomato and strawberries; spoon on top of soup. Sprinkle with goat cheese and the 2 tablespoons small basil leaves; drizzle with the remaining 2 teaspoons oil.

tips You could use red wine vinegar instead of sherry vinegar. For a canape, serve gazpacho in shot glasses.

chile paprika pasta with fresh tomato sauce

PREP + COOK TIME 50 MINUTES
(+ REFRIGERATION & STANDING)
SERVES 4

2½ CUPS SPELT FLOUR,
PLUS MORE FOR DUSTING

1 TEASPOON CHILE POWDER

1 TEASPOON RED PEPPER FLAKES

1 TABLESPOON SMOKED PAPRIKA

½ TEASPOON SALT

2 EGGS, AT ROOM TEMPERATURE

¼ CUP WATER

¼ CUP PLUS 2 TABLESPOONS OLIVE OIL

1¼ POUNDS MIXED TOMATO MEDLEY,
HALVED OR CHOPPED

1 TEASPOON FINELY GRATED LEMON ZEST

1 CLOVE GARLIC, CRUSHED

2 TABLESPOONS RED WINE VINEGAR

2 TEASPOONS HONEY

2 TABLESPOONS CHOPPED FRESH CHIVES

2 OUNCES RICOTTA SALATA, CRUMBLED

1 Combine flour, chile powder, pepper flakes, paprika, and salt in a large bowl. Make a well in the center. Whisk eggs, the water, and 2 tablespoons oil in a medium bowl; pour into well. Use a fork to slowly incorporate the egg mixture into the flour mixture; mix to a dough. Turn dough onto a lightly floured surface; knead for 10 minutes or until smooth and pliable. Wrap in plastic wrap; refrigerate for 1 hour.
2 Combine tomatoes, zest, garlic, the ¼ cup oil, the vinegar, honey, and half the chives in a large nonreactive bowl; season to taste. Let stand for 30 minutes.
3 Divide dough into quarters; dust lightly with extra flour. Roll each portion through a pasta machine set on the thickest setting. Fold dough in half, roll through machine. Repeat rolling several times, adjusting the setting so the pasta sheets become thinner with each roll. Roll to the third thinnest setting. Hang sheets for 10 minutes to dry slightly. Loosely fold or roll pasta sheets; cut into ¾-inch strips. Dust lightly with a little extra flour.
4 Cook pasta in a large saucepan of boiling salted water, uncovered, for 2 minutes or until just tender; drain. Add pasta to tomato mixture; toss to combine. Serve topped with ricotta and remaining chives.

tips The pasta dough can be mixed in a food processor. You can use superfine sugar instead of honey in the fresh tomato sauce. If you can't find salted ricotta, you can use fresh ricotta, feta, or goat cheese.
make ahead You can make the pasta dough a day ahead; keep wrapped in plastic wrap in the fridge. Stand dough at room temperature for at least 30 minutes before rolling through the pasta machine.

shrimp salad with sriracha tofu dressing

PREP TIME 15 MINUTES

SERVES 4

1 POUND LARGE COOKED SHRIMP

4 OUNCES SILKEN TOFU, DRAINED, CRUMBLED

2 SMALL RED BELL PEPPERS, SLICED THINLY

2 TABLESPOONS RICE WINE VINEGAR

1 TABLESPOON SRIRACHA SAUCE

1 TABLESPOON HONEY

2 TEASPOONS WHITE (SHIRO) MISO PASTE

1 LARGE ZUCCHINI, CUT INTO LONG THIN STRIPS

1 BUNCH RED RADISHES, TRIMMED, SLICED THINLY

1 TABLESPOON FINELY CHOPPED PICKLED GINGER

¼ CUP TOASTED PEANUTS

MICRO RED SHISHO LEAVES, TO SERVE

1 Shell and devein shrimp, leaving tails intact.

2 Place tofu, ¼ cup of the sliced bell pepper, the vinegar, sriracha, honey, and miso in a food processor or blender; pulse until smooth.

3 Place remaining bell pepper in a large bowl with zucchini, radish, and ginger; toss gently to combine. Top with shrimp and peanuts; drizzle with dressing, sprinkle with shisho leaves.

make ahead The dressing can be made several hours ahead; keep refrigerated.

Tuna crudo with red endive & pickled red onion

PREP TIME 20 MINUTES
SERVES 4 AS A STARTER

½ SMALL RED ONION, SLICED THINLY

1 SMALL CLOVE GARLIC, CHOPPED FINELY

¼ CUP RUBY GRAPEFRUIT JUICE

1 TABLESPOON LEMON JUICE

1 TABLESPOON RED WINE VINEGAR

½ TEASPOON CRUSHED PINK PEPPERCORNS

¼ CUP OLIVE OIL

1 RUBY GRAPEFRUIT

2 RED BELGIAN ENDIVE, LEAVES SEPARATED

¾ POUND SASHIMI-GRADE TUNA, SLICED THINLY

2 TABLESPOONS BULL'S BLOOD CRESS (OR MICRO CHARD OR RED GARNET)

1 Place onion and garlic in a medium nonreactive bowl; add juices and vinegar. Let stand for 5 minutes or until softened. Drain onion mixture over a pitcher or bowl; reserve liquid.
2 To make dressing, add peppercorns and oil to reserved liquid in pitcher; season to taste.
3 Meanwhile, segment grapefruit by removing the peel thickly so no white pith remains. Cut between membranes, over a bowl to catch any juice, releasing segments. You will need half the segments for this recipe; reserve remaining segments for another use.
4 Arrange endive, tuna, grapefruit, and onion mixture on a platter; drizzle with dressing. Sprinkle with cress.

tip It is important to have very fresh, high-quality tuna for this recipe. Try to buy it on the day of serving.
make ahead This recipe can be prepared to the end of step 3, several hours ahead; keep refrigerated. Slice tuna and assemble close to serving.

rhubarb-glazed chickens with radicchio slaw

PREP + COOK TIME
1 HOUR 15 MINUTES
SERVES 4

4 X 1-POUND SMALL CHICKENS

2 RADICCHIO HEARTS,
LEAVES SEPARATED

⅓ CUP TOASTED PECANS,
CHOPPED COARSELY

⅓ CUP DRIED CRANBERRIES, CHOPPED
COARSELY

¼ CUP LEMON JUICE

⅓ CUP EXTRA-VIRGIN OLIVE OIL

RHUBARB GLAZE

⅓ CUP OLIVE OIL

3 CUPS COARSELY CHOPPED RHUBARB
(SEE TIP)

1 SMALL RED ONION, SLICED THINLY

2 CLOVES GARLIC, CRUSHED

½ CUP PASSATA (TOMATO PASTA SAUCE)

⅓ CUP APPLE CIDER VINEGAR

⅓ CUP HONEY

1½ TABLESPOONS SMOKED PAPRIKA

1 Make rhubarb glaze. Reserve half the glaze for serving.

2 Preheat the oven to 350°F. Line two large baking sheets with parchment paper.

3 Rinse chickens and pat them dry inside and out. Use kitchen scissors to cut along each side of the backbone; discard backbone. Turn chickens over and press firmly on the breast to flatten. Brush chickens all over with some of the remaining glaze.

4 Cook chickens, breast-side down, on a heated oiled grill pan (or on a grill or under a broiler) over medium-high heat for 1 minute or until grill marks appear. Transfer to the prepared baking sheets. Brush generously with remaining glaze. Roast for 25 minutes or until cooked through. Cover; rest for 5 minutes.

5 Meanwhile, place radicchio and pecans in a large bowl. Place cranberries, juice, and oil in a screw-top jar; shake well. Pour dressing over salad, season; toss gently to combine.

6 Serve chickens with radicchio slaw and reserved glaze.

rhubarb glaze Heat oil in a medium saucepan over medium heat; cook rhubarb, onion, and garlic, stirring, for 5 minutes or until softened. Add remaining ingredients; simmer over low heat for 20 minutes, stirring occasionally, or until thickened. Cool 5 minutes. Blend or process until smooth; season to taste.

tip You will need about 6 fresh rhubarb stems.

make ahead Rhubarb glaze can be made up to 3 days ahead. Keep covered in the fridge.

vietnamese tomato & chile fish soup

PREP + COOK TIME 35 MINUTES

SERVES 4

6 CUPS VEGETABLE STOCK

2 TABLESPOONS FISH SAUCE

2 TABLESPOONS FIRMLY PACKED
BROWN SUGAR

2 CLOVES GARLIC, SLICED THINLY

2 STALKS FRESH LEMONGRASS, BRUISED

4 RED SHALLOTS, SLICED THINLY

1¼ POUNDS FIRM WHITE FISH FILLETS, CUT
INTO ¾-INCH CUBES

3 MEDIUM VINE-RIPENED TOMATOES, CUT
INTO THIN WEDGES

2 FRESH LONG RED CHILES, SLICED THINLY

1 TABLESPOON LIME JUICE

3 OUNCES BEAN SPROUTS

½ CUP LOOSELY PACKED FRESH
VIETNAMESE MINT LEAVES

½ CUP LOOSELY PACKED FRESH CILANTRO
LEAVES

1 Combine stock, sauce, sugar, garlic, lemongrass, and shallot in a large saucepan; bring to a boil. Reduce heat to low; simmer, uncovered, for 20 minutes.

2 Add fish, tomatoes, and chile; cook for 2 minutes or until fish is just cooked through. Stir in lime juice. Discard lemongrass. Season to taste.

3 Divide soup between bowls. Top with bean sprouts and herbs.

tips Use sustainable fish for this recipe—ling is used here. Fish will continue to cook in the hot broth so don't overcook it in step 2. Add noodles to soup for a more hearty meal.

paprika & cumin spiced chicken

PREP + COOK TIME 45 MINUTES
SERVES 4

4 CLOVES GARLIC, CRUSHED

1 TABLESPOON SMOKED PAPRIKA

1 TEASPOON CUMIN SEEDS

½ CUP OLIVE OIL

½ CUP GREEK-STYLE YOGURT

4 X 6½-OUNCE CHICKEN BREAST SUPREMES
(SEE TIP)

1 CAN (15 OZ) CHICKPEAS, DRAINED,
RINSED

¾ POUND CHERRY TOMATOES

1¼ CUPS FIRM RICOTTA,
BROKEN INTO LARGE CHUNKS

½ CUP LOOSELY PACKED CILANTRO SPRIGS

1 Preheat the oven to 475°F. Line a large shallow baking dish with parchment paper.
2 Combine garlic, paprika, cumin, and ⅓ cup of the oil in a small bowl. Combine yogurt and 2 teaspoons of the spice oil mixture in another small bowl; season. Cover yogurt mixture; refrigerate until required.
3 Rub 2 tablespoons of the remaining spice oil mixture over chicken; season. Heat remaining oil in a large frying pan over high heat; cook chicken for 2 minutes each side or until browned. Transfer chicken to baking dish. Roast chicken for 10 minutes.
4 Reduce oven to 400°F. Combine chickpeas, tomatoes, ricotta, and remaining spice oil mixture in a large bowl. Spoon chickpea mixture around chicken in dish; season. Roast for a further 15 minutes or until chicken is cooked through.
5 Serve chicken and chickpea mixture with yogurt sauce, sprinkled with coriander.

tip Chicken supremes are chicken breasts with the skin on and wing bone still attached. They are available from most butcher stores; you may need to order them in advance.

chicken bake with rhubarb, bell pepper & chile

PREP + COOK TIME

1 HOUR 10 MINUTES (+ STANDING)

SERVES 4

¼ CUP MAPLE SYRUP

1 TABLESPOON TOMATO PASTE

1 CLOVE GARLIC, CRUSHED

1 TEASPOON SMOKED PAPRIKA

4 CHICKEN MARYLANDS

1 POUND CHERRY TOMATOES

2–3 LARGE RED BELL PEPPERS, SLICED
THICKLY

1 MEDIUM RED ONION,
CUT INTO WEDGES

¾ POUND RHUBARB, TRIMMED, CUT INTO
2-INCH LENGTHS

4 FRESH LARGE RED CHILES, HALVED
LENGTHWISE, SEEDS REMOVED

8 SPRIGS FRESH OREGANO

1 CUP RED RICE

2 CUPS WATER

1 Combine syrup, paste, garlic, and paprika in a large bowl; season. Add chicken; toss to coat. Let stand for 30 minutes.

2 Meanwhile, preheat the oven to 350°F. Line a large rimmed baking sheet with parchment paper.

3 Remove chicken pieces from marinade; reserve marinade. Place chicken on prepared baking sheet. Place tomatoes, bell peppers, onion, rhubarb, chiles, and oregano around chicken; season. Roast for 30 minutes. Brush chicken with reserved marinade. Bake for a further 20 minutes or until chicken is cooked through and vegetables are tender.

4 Meanwhile, wash rice in sieve under cold water until water runs clear; drain. Place rice in a medium saucepan with the water; bring to a boil. Reduce heat; simmer, covered, for 35 minutes. Remove from heat; stand, covered, for 10 minutes. Fluff grains with a fork.

5 Serve chicken with roast vegetables and rice.

tip Marylands are the joined thigh and leg section. You can use 4 thighs on the bone and 4 drumsticks, if you prefer.

vegetable black rice "paella"

PREP + COOK TIME
1 HOUR 15 MINUTES
SERVES 4

1 TEASPOON SMOKED PAPRIKA

1 TEASPOON SWEET PAPRIKA

½ TEASPOON CHILE POWDER

LARGE PINCH SAFFRON THREADS

¼ CUP BOILING WATER

¼ CUP OLIVE OIL

2 CLOVES GARLIC, CHOPPED FINELY

1 MEDIUM RED ONION,
CHOPPED FINELY

2 LARGE RED BELL PEPPERS, CHOPPED
COARSELY

¾ POUND CHERRY TOMATOES

1 LARGE EGGPLANT,
CHOPPED COARSELY

1 CUP BLACK RICE, RINSED

2¼ CUPS VEGETABLE STOCK

2 CUPS WATER

8 MARINATED ARTICHOKE HALVES

2 TABLESPOONS FRESH FLAT-LEAF
PARSLEY LEAVES

1 Combine both paprikas and chile powder in a small bowl. Place saffron in another small bowl; cover with the boiling water.

2 Heat half the oil in a 9-inch paella pan or large deep frying pan over high heat. Cook half the spice mixture, stirring, for 30 seconds or until fragrant. Add garlic, onion, and bell peppers; cook, stirring, for 3 minutes or until onion is lightly golden. Add tomatoes; cook for 10 minutes, mashing the tomatoes slightly with a wooden spoon until tomatoes begin to break down. Remove from pan.

3 Add remaining oil and spices to same pan; cook, stirring, for 30 seconds or until fragrant. Add eggplant; cook, stirring, for 5 minutes or until eggplant is softened.

4 Add rice; cook, stirring, for 2 minutes. Stir in stock, the 2 cups water, saffron mixture, and bell pepper mixture; bring to a boil. Reduce heat to medium; simmer, uncovered, stirring occasionally, for 40 minutes or until most of the liquid is absorbed and the rice is tender.

5 Arrange artichokes on rice; cook, covered, for 5 minutes or until heated through.

6 Serve paella topped with parsley.

make ahead The mixture can be prepared to the end of step 3 a day ahead.

duck, raspberry & cilantro salad

PREP + COOK TIME 25 MINUTES
SERVES 4

2 LARGE DUCK BREAST FILLETS

3 OUNCES BABY LEAF SALAD
WITH BEET LEAVES

¼ CUP TOASTED CASHEWS

½ CUP LOOSELY PACKED FRESH CILANTRO
LEAVES

4 OUNCES RASPBERRIES

TAMARI DRESSING

¼ CUP LIME JUICE

1½ TEASPOONS HONEY

½ TEASPOON SESAME OIL

3 TEASPOONS TAMARI

1 Preheat the oven to 400°F.

2 Pat duck breasts dry with paper towels. Lightly score the skin in a crisscross pattern. Season skin with salt. Place duck, skin-side down, in a cold ovenproof frying pan over medium heat. Once duck has begun to sizzle, cook for 5 minutes or until skin is golden. Turn; cook for 1 minute. Transfer pan to oven; roast, uncovered, for a further 6 minutes or until cooked to your liking. Duck breast is best served slightly rare in the center. Remove from pan; rest, covered, for 5 minutes. Slice duck breasts diagonally.

3 Meanwhile, make tamari dressing.

4 Serve duck with salad leaves, cashews, cilantro, and raspberries; drizzle with dressing.

tamari dressing Whisk ingredients in a small pitcher.

tips If you don't have an ovenproof frying pan, use a flameproof baking dish or transfer the duck to a baking dish after pan-frying. You can use chicken breast fillets in place of duck; roast until just cooked through. For a shortcut, buy a barbecued duck from an Asian foods store and break the meat off in chunks. Placing the duck in a cold pan and bringing up to the heat gives the duck a longer opportunity to render the fat from the skin without overcooking the meat.

make ahead Dressing can be made a day ahead.

harissa beef fillet with almonds & pomegranate

PREP + COOK TIME
40 MINUTES (+ STANDING)
SERVES 4

1½-POUND BEEF FILLET

1 TABLESPOON OLIVE OIL

2 TABLESPOONS ALMONDS, TOASTED, CHOPPED COARSELY

¼ CUP POMEGRANATE SEEDS

2 TABLESPOONS MIXED MICRO RADISH LEAVES OR RED GARNET

HARISSA PASTE

½ TEASPOON CUMIN SEEDS

½ TEASPOON CORIANDER SEEDS

4 FRESH LONG RED CHILES, CHOPPED

2 CLOVES GARLIC, CHOPPED

¾-INCH PIECE FRESH GINGER, PEELED, GRATED

2 TABLESPOONS OLIVE OIL

1 TABLESPOON LEMON JUICE

POMEGRANATE MOLASSES DRESSING

¼ CUP LEMON JUICE

2 TABLESPOONS POMEGRANATE MOLASSES

1 TABLESPOON OLIVE OIL

1 Preheat the oven to 400°F.

2 Make harissa paste.

3 Trim any silver skin or fat from fillet. Coat fillet in harissa paste. Heat oil in a large nonstick frying pan over medium-high heat; cook fillet, turning, for 3 minutes or until browned all over. Transfer to a baking dish; roast for 20 minutes for medium-rare or until cooked to your liking (see tips for using a meat thermometer). Transfer to a plate; cover loosely with foil, rest for 10 minutes.

4 Meanwhile, place almonds in a single layer on a baking sheet; roast for 3 minutes or until golden.

5 Make pomegranate molasses dressing.

6 Slice fillet thickly; arrange slices on plates. Drizzle with dressing; top with almonds, pomegranate seeds, and micro herbs.

harissa paste Toast seeds in a small frying pan over medium heat for 2 minutes, shaking pan occasionally, or until fragrant. Transfer seeds to a small food processor. Add remaining ingredients; process until mixture forms a paste. Season with salt.

pomegranate molasses dressing Place ingredients in a screw-top jar; shake well. Season to taste.

tip A meat thermometer takes the guesswork out of roasting. Some thermometers are inserted at the beginning of cooking and some are used at the end—check the package for instructions. For beef fillet, insert thermometer into the center of the thickest part. Cook beef until it reaches 140°F for rare, 150-158°F for medium, and 167°F for well done.

make ahead Harissa paste can be made up to 3 days ahead; store, covered, in the fridge.

serving suggestion This recipe can be served warm, or cooled with salad leaves.

red quinoa salad with sweet & sour bell pepper

PREP + COOK TIME 30 MINUTES
SERVES 4

1 CUP RED QUINOA

2 CUPS WATER

2 TABLESPOONS OLIVE OIL

1 MEDIUM RED ONION,
SLICED THICKLY

2 LARGE RED BELL PEPPERS, SLICED
THICKLY

2 CLOVES GARLIC, SLICED

2 TABLESPOONS FRESH LEMON
THYME LEAVES

¼ CUP GOLDEN RAISINS

¼ CUP RED WINE VINEGAR

¼ CUP HONEY

½ CUP COARSELY CHOPPED
TOASTED WALNUTS

3 OUNCES FETA, CRUMBLED

½ CUP LOOSELY PACKED FRESH
MINT LEAVES

1 Place quinoa and the water in a medium saucepan; bring to a boil. Reduce heat to low; cook, covered, for 15 minutes or until quinoa is tender. Fluff quinoa with a fork.

2 Meanwhile, heat oil in a large frying pan over medium heat; cook onion, bell peppers, garlic, and thyme, stirring occasionally, for 15 minutes or until softened. Add sultanas, vinegar, and honey; cook, stirring, for 1 minute or until combined and well coated. Season to taste.

3 Place quinoa and bell pepper mixture in a large bowl; toss gently to combine. Serve warm or at room temperature, topped with walnuts, feta, and mint.

make ahead Sweet and sour bell pepper mixture can be made a day ahead; reheat gently before serving.

serving suggestion Serve with grilled meat or chicken.

Red and orange tomatoes, but not yellow and green, contain the carotenoid lycopene, an antioxidant that gives them their red color.

They also trump yellow tomatoes with extra fiber, more vitamin C, and vitamin A; the latter protects our eyes. But yellow tomatoes hold their worth in other areas (see right). Although cooking tomatoes reduces the vitamin C content it helps with lycopene absorption. Tomato paste is a significantly rich source, especially when paired with extra-virgin oil, since lycopene is fat-soluble. Lycopene is associated with a lower risk of macular degeneration, several types of significant cancers (prostate, skin, and cervical), and may help reduce your risk of coronary artery disease.

All tomatoes great and small

The recipes in this chapter focus on red types, from large meaty heirloom oxheart tomatoes to sweet teardrop types. Yellow tomatoes surpass their red cousins in several areas, with almost double the iron, zinc, niacin, and folate. Green heirloom tomatoes also stack up well next to reds, with more vitamin C and calcium, and many similar nutrients, but are significantly higher in tomatine, which may fight breast, colon, stomach, and liver cancer cells.

Ripen and store large tomatoes at room temperature; refrigeration can dull the flavor. Ripened tomatoes for cooking can be stored in the fridge.

SMOKY ROAST TOMATOES WITH TOFU TOAST

Whisk ⅓ cup extra-virgin olive oil, 3 crushed garlic cloves, 1 tablespoon smoked paprika, 1 teaspoon each sweet paprika, ground cumin, and salt, and ¼ teaspoon red pepper flakes. Toss 12 oz cherry heirloom tomatoes and 12½ oz chickpeas with half the oil mix in a roasting pan. Cook at 425°F for 20 minutes, until tomatoes soften. Meanwhile, thickly slice a 12-oz block of firm tofu, pat dry, pressing down well on tofu. Brush with remaining oil mix; pan-fry each side until golden. Serve with tomato mixture, yogurt, and cilantro.

Easy ways to use up ripe tomatoes

Do as the Spanish do! Grill two slices of rustic bread, rubbed with garlic, drizzled with oil. Rub tomato halves onto the toasted bread until all pulp is absorbed and only the skin remains; season.

Dice and combine tomato in a bowl with 1 tablespoon each finely chopped red onion and cilantro, and as much chopped jalapeño chile as your dare, for a zippy authentic Mexican salsa. Throw into any number of soupy, stewy, or pasta-type dishes.

spiced rhubarb jellies with vanilla bean yogurt

PREP + COOK TIME

30 MINUTES (+ REFRIGERATION)

SERVES 4

⅓ CUP CRÈME DE CASSIS

⅓ CUP WATER

⅓ CUP RAW SUGAR

---

2 WHOLE CLOVES

---

1 STAR ANISE

---

1 CINNAMON STICK

---

1 STRIP LEMON PEEL

---

2 TEASPOONS VANILLA BEAN PASTE

⅓ POUND RHUBARB, SLICED THINLY

---

2 TEASPOONS POWDERED GELATIN

½ CUP GREEK-STYLE YOGURT

---

1 TABLESPOON TRIMMED RED GARNET
(OR OTHER RED MICRO HERBS)

---

1 Stir liqueur, the water, sugar, spices, lemon peel, and half the vanilla paste in a medium saucepan over medium heat; bring to a boil. Reduce heat to low; simmer, uncovered, for 5 minutes. Discard spices and peel. Add rhubarb; simmer, uncovered, for 2 minutes or until tender. Sprinkle in gelatin; stir until dissolved. Cool to room temperature.

2 Pour half the rhubarb mixture into four 1-cup glasses.
Cover; refrigerate for 2 hours or until set.

3 Pour remaining rhubarb mixture over set mixture in glasses.
Cover; refrigerate for another 2 hours or overnight.

4 Combine yogurt with remaining vanilla paste in a small bowl.

5 Serve rhubarb jellies topped with vanilla bean yogurt and micro herbs.

tip Crème de cassis is a blackcurrant liqueur.

make ahead The jellies can be made a day ahead.

strawberry & raspberry galette

PREP + COOK TIME
1 HOUR 10 MINUTES
(+ REFRIGERATION)
SERVES 8

¾ CUP ALL-PURPOSE FLOUR

¾ CUP RYE FLOUR

½ CUP GROUND ALMONDS

5½ OUNCES CHILLED BUTTER, CHOPPED
COARSELY

½ CUP PLUS 2 TEASPOONS SUPERFINE
SUGAR

---

3 TEASPOONS CRUSHED DRIED
PINK PEPPERCORNS

---

2 EGGS, EACH BEATEN LIGHTLY IN
SEPARATE BOWLS

---

1 TEASPOON ICED WATER, APPROXIMATELY

---

1 POUND SMALL STRAWBERRIES

¾ POUND FRESH RASPBERRIES

---

1 Sift plain and rye flours into a large bowl; stir in half the ground almonds. Rub in butter until mixture is crumbly; stir in ⅓ cup of the ½ cup sugar and 2 teaspoons of the peppercorns. Add 1 beaten egg and enough of the iced water to make ingredients just come together. Knead dough gently on a lightly floured surface until smooth. Wrap in plastic wrap; refrigerate for 1 hour.
2 Preheat the oven to 400°F; place a large baking sheet in the oven while preheating.
3 Roll dough between sheets of parchment paper into a 12-inch round. Sprinkle pastry with remaining ground almonds, leaving a 1½-inch border.
4 Combine strawberries, ½ pound raspberries, and remaining sugar of the ½ cup sugar in a medium bowl. Pile fruit on ground almonds on pastry. Fold pastry edge over filling, pleating and pinching to create a rustic edge. Brush pastry edge with remaining beaten egg; sprinkle with the 2 teaspoons sugar and remaining peppercorns.
5 Slide pie, on parchment paper, onto preheated baking sheet. Bake for 35 minutes or until pastry is browned. Cover loosely with foil if pastry is over-browning before it is crisp.
6 Serve pie topped with remaining ¼ pound raspberries.

tip The rye flour and ground almonds give a more tender, crumbly texture to the pastry.
make ahead Pastry can be made to the end of step 1 a day ahead.
serving suggestion Serve with the raspberry ripple yogurt mixture from Raspberry Ripple Yogurt Pops, page 228.

coconut red rice pudding with roasted cherries

PREP + COOK TIME
1 HOUR 10 MINUTES
SERVES 4

- 1 CUP RED RICE
- 2½ CUPS CANNED COCONUT MILK
- 2 CUPS WATER
- ⅓ CUP PLUS ¼ CUP MAPLE SYRUP
- 1 TEASPOON VANILLA BEAN PASTE
- ¼ TEASPOON SALT
- 1 STAR ANISE
- ¾ POUND CHERRIES
- ½ CUP FLAKED COCONUT, TOASTED

1 Place rice, 2 cups coconut milk, the water, ¼ cup maple syrup, the vanilla paste, salt, and star anise in a medium saucepan over medium heat; bring to a simmer. Reduce heat to low; simmer, uncovered, stirring occasionally, for 55 minutes or until rice is tender. Discard star anise.

2 Meanwhile, preheat the oven to 350°F. Line a baking sheet with parchment paper. Combine cherries and 2 tablespoons of the maple syrup in a medium bowl; place cherry mixture on prepared baking sheet. Bake for 20 minutes or until cherries are soft and bubbling.

3 Combine the remaining ½ cup coconut milk and remaining maple syrup in a small pitcher.

4 Serve warm rice pudding topped with roasted cherries, flaked coconut, and maple coconut milk mixture.

make ahead Recipe is best made on day of serving. If made ahead, the pudding will become thicker on standing; reheat gently with a little extra coconut milk.

baked ricotta cheesecakes with poached tamarillos

PREP + COOK TIME 1 HOUR
(+ COOLING & REFRIGERATION)
SERVES 6

1¼ CUPS GROUND ALMONDS

⅓ CUP PLUS ¼ CUP RAPADURA SUGAR (SEE TIPS) OR SUPERFINE SUGAR

2 TEASPOONS FINELY GRATED LEMON ZEST

¼ POUND BUTTER, MELTED

1 VANILLA BEAN

1 POUND FIRM RICOTTA

⅓ CUP GREEK-STYLE YOGURT

2 EGGS

POACHED TAMARILLOS

½ CUP SUPERFINE SUGAR

½ CUP RAPADURA SUGAR

1 CUP WATER

1 STAR ANISE

1 VANILLA BEAN, SPLIT LENGTHWISE

4 TAMARILLOS

1 Preheat the oven to 350°F.

2 Combine ground almonds, ¼ cup of the sugar, the zest, and butter in a medium bowl. Press mixture over the base of six greased 3-inch nonstick loose-based dessert pans. Place pans on a baking sheet. Bake bases for 6 minutes or until browned lightly. Cool.

3 Split vanilla bean in half lengthwise; scrape seeds into food processor. Add ricotta, yogurt, the remaining ⅓ cup sugar, and eggs; process until combined. Pour mixture over base in pans.

4 Bake cheesecakes for 15 minutes or until almost set in the center. Turn off the oven; leave in oven with the door ajar for 1 hour. Cool. Refrigerate for 3 hours before serving.

5 Meanwhile, make poached tamarillos.

6 Serve cheesecakes toppd with poached tamarillo halves and syrup.

poached tamarillos Place sugars, the water, star anise, and vanilla bean in a medium saucepan. Cut 1 tamarillo in half; squeeze juice from tamarillo. Add juice to pan; stir over medium heat until sugar dissolves. Bring just to a boil. Cut remaining tamarillos three-quarters of the way through. Add to pan; simmer, uncovered, for 4 minutes. Remove tamarillos from syrup with a slotted spoon, to a bowl. Return syrup to a boil; boil, uncovered, for 6 minutes or until thickened slightly. Strain syrup; discard solids. Cool. Cut tamarillos in half lengthwise.

tips Rapadura sugar, also known as panela, is an unrefined sugar available at well-stocked supermarkets and health-food stores. You can use any unrefined sugar you prefer. You can use plums or cherries in place of the tamarillos; reduce the cooking time to 2 minutes for cherries.

make ahead Cheesecakes and poached tamarillos can be made a day ahead; refrigerate in separate containers.

rhubarb & walnut tart

PREP + COOK TIME 45 MINUTES
(+ REFRIGERATION & COOLING)
SERVES 8

IT WILL BE EASIER TO FINELY GRATE THE
ZEST FROM THE ORANGE BEFORE YOU
SQUEEZE THE JUICE.

6 STEMS RHUBARB, WASHED

¼ CUP WATER

¼ CUP ORANGE JUICE

⅓ CUP RAPADURA SUGAR (SEE TIPS)

½ TEASPOON GROUND CARDAMOM

1 TEASPOON FINELY GRATED ORANGE ZEST

COOKING-OIL SPRAY

3 CUPS WALNUTS

4 FRESH DATES, PITTED

1 TABLESPOON COCONUT OIL, MELTED

1 EGG WHITE

HONEY CRÈME PATISSIERE

1 VANILLA BEAN

2 CUPS MILK

4 EGG YOLKS

⅓ CUP HONEY

⅓ CUP ALL-PURPOSE SPELT FLOUR

1 Preheat the oven to 350°F. Trim ends of rhubarb; cut stems into 4¾-inch lengths. Place rhubarb in a medium ovenproof dish with the water, juice, sugar, cardamom, and zest; stir to coat. Roast for 15 minutes; cool. Refrigerate until cold.
2 Make honey crème patissiere.
3 Coat a 5 x 14–inch loose-based flan tin with cooking-oil spray. Process walnuts and dates to a fine crumb. Add coconut oil and egg white; pulse to combine. Press crumb mixture evenly on base and side of flan tin; bake for 10 minutes. Cool in tin. Remove from tin; place on a platter.
4 Spoon crème patissiere into tart case; top with rhubarb, drizzle with rhubarb juices.

honey crème patissiere Split vanilla bean lengthwise; scrape out seeds. Combine vanilla bean and seeds, and milk in a small saucepan. Bring to a boil over a medium heat; let stand for 5 minutes. Whisk egg yolks, honey and flour in a medium saucepan. Gradually whisk in strained hot milk. Cook, stirring, over medium heat for 5 minutes or until mixture boils and thickens. Transfer to a medium heatproof bowl; place plastic wrap directly on surface of crème patissiere. Cool for 20 minutes (see tips); refrigerate until cold.

tips Rapadura is an unrefined sugar, available at well-stocked supermarkets and health-food stores. You can use coconut sugar instead. If the crème patissiere is lumpy after cooking, push it through a fine sieve. To cool crème patissiere quickly, place the bowl in a larger bowl of ice, stirring frequently until cooled. Remaining egg whites can be kept to make meringue or added to omelets and frittatas; refrigerate, covered, for up to 3 days or place in a small airtight container and freeze for up to 3 months. You can also top this tart with roasted pears or apples, or fresh raspberries.

raspberry ripple yogurt pops

PREP + COOK TIME
15 MINUTES (+ FREEZING)
MAKES 6

YOU WILL NEED TO BEGIN THIS RECIPE A DAY AHEAD. YOU WILL NEED 6 POP STICKS. IT WILL BE EASIER TO FINELY GRATE THE ZEST FROM THE LEMON BEFORE YOU SQUEEZE THE JUICE.

¼ POUND FRESH OR FROZEN RASPBERRIES

1 TABLESPOON LEMON JUICE

2 TABLESPOONS HONEY

1 VANILLA BEAN

1 CUP GREEK-STYLE YOGURT

1 TEASPOON FINELY GRATED LEMON ZEST

1 Place raspberries, juice, and 2 tablespoons honey in a medium bowl; crush berries using a fork. Spoon 1 tablespoon of the raspberry mixture into the base of each of six ⅓-cup dariole molds or paper cups. Freeze for 1 hour or until firm.
2 Meanwhile, split vanilla bean in half lengthwise; scrape seeds into medium bowl. Whisk in yogurt, zest, and remaining 1½ tablespoons honey until combined. Fold in remaining raspberry mixture to form a ripple effect.
3 Divide mixture among molds; insert a pop stick into each. Freeze overnight.
4 Dip molds quickly in hot water; turn out.

make ahead Pops can be made up to a week ahead.

melt-and-mix strawberry yogurt cake

PREP + COOK TIME
1 HOUR 15 MINUTES
(+ STANDING & COOLING)
SERVES 8

2½ CUPS SELF-RISING FLOUR

½ POUND STRAWBERRIES, CHOPPED
COARSELY

⅔ CUP SUPERFINE SUGAR

1 TEASPOON VANILLA BEAN PASTE

2 EGGS, BEATEN LIGHTLY

1½ CUP GREEK-STYLE YOGURT

⅓ CUP UNSALTED BUTTER, MELTED

½ CUP TOASTED ALMONDS,
SLICED THINLY

MACERATED STRAWBERRIES

½ POUND STRAWBERRIES,
HALVED OR QUARTERED

1 TABLESPOON LEMON JUICE

1 TABLESPOON SUPERFINE SUGAR

1 Preheat the oven to 350°F. Line base and side of a 9-inch springform pan with parchment paper.
2 Sift flour into a bowl; stir in strawberries, sugar, vanilla paste, egg, ½ cup yogurt, and butter until just combined. Spoon mixture into pan; smooth the surface. Sprinkle with almonds.
3 Bake cake for 50 minutes or until a skewer inserted into the center comes out clean. Leave cake in pan for 10 minutes. Release ring; transfer cake to a wire rack to cool.
4 Meanwhile, make macerated strawberries.
5 Serve cake topped with macerated strawberries and remaining 1 cup yogurt.
macerated strawberries Combine ingredients in a small bowl; let stand for 20 minutes.

tip Cake and macerated strawberries are best made on day of serving.

watermelon & cherry salad

PREP + COOK TIME
20 MINUTES (+ COOLING)
SERVES 4

½ POUND FRESH CHERRIES, PITTED

¼ POUND FRESH RASPBERRIES

1¼ POUNDS WATERMELON,
SLICED THINLY

⅓ CUP POMEGRANATE SEEDS

ROSE WATER & CITRUS SYRUP

1 TEASPOON FINELY GRATED
ORANGE ZEST

2 TABLESPOONS ORANGE JUICE

1 TABLESPOON LIME JUICE

1 CUP WATER

1 CUP SUPERFINE SUGAR

1 TEASPOON ROSE WATER

1 Make rose water and citrus syrup.

2 Arrange fruit on a platter; drizzle with syrup just before serving.

rose water & citrus syrup Combine zest, juices, the water, and sugar in a medium saucepan. Stir over medium heat, without boiling, until sugar dissolves. Bring to a boil; boil, uncovered, for 8 minutes or until thickened slightly. Stir in rose water; cool.

make ahead Syrup can be made up to 3 days ahead; keep refrigerated.

Glossary

AGAVE SYRUP from the agave plant; has a low GI, but that is due to the high percentage of fructose present, which may be harmful in large quantities.

ALMONDS

blanched brown skins removed.

flaked paper-thin slices.

ground also called almond meal.

ARTICHOKE large flower-bud of a member of the thistle family; it has tough petal-like leaves, and is edible in part when cooked.

hearts tender center of the globe artichoke; can be harvested from the plant after the prickly choke is removed. Cooked hearts can be purchased or canned in brine.

BAKING POWDER a rising agent consisting mainly of two parts cream of tartar to one part baking soda (bicarbonate of soda).

BAKING SODA (BICARBONATE OF SODA) a rising agent.

BARLEY a nutritious grain used in soups and stews. Hulled barley, the least processed, is high in fiber. Pearl barley has had the husk removed then been steamed and polished so that only the "pearl" of the original grain remains, much the same as white rice.

BEANS

black also called turtle beans or black kidney beans; an earthy-flavored dried bean completely different from Chinese black beans (fermented soybeans). Used mostly in Mexican and South American cooking.

cannellini a small white bean similar in appearance and flavor to other white beans (great northern, navy or haricot), all of which can be substituted for the other. Available dried or canned.

fava available dried, fresh, canned, and frozen. Fresh should be peeled twice (discarding both the outer long green pod and the beige-green tough inner shell); the frozen beans have had their pods removed but the beige shell still needs removal.

white a generic term used for canned or dried cannellini, haricot, navy, or great northern beans, as they belong to the same family.

BEETS firm, round root vegetable.

BELL PEPPER comes in many colors: red, green, yellow, orange and purplish-black. Be sure to discard seeds and membranes before use.

BROCCOLINI a cross between broccoli and Chinese kale; it has long asparagus-like stems with a long loose floret, both are edible. Resembles broccoli but is milder and sweeter in taste.

BUTTER use salted or unsalted (sweet) butter; one stick of butter is equal to 8 tablespoons.

BUTTERMILK originally the term given to the slightly sour liquid left after butter was churned from cream, today it is made from no-fat or low-fat milk to which specific bacterial cultures have been added. Despite its name, it is actually low in fat.

CAPERS grey-green buds of a warm climate shrub (usually Mediterranean), sold either dried and salted or pickled in a vinegar brine. Capers must be rinsed well before using.

CARDAMOM a spice native to India and used extensively in its cuisine; can be purchased in pod, seed, or ground form. Has a distinctive aromatic, sweetly rich flavor.

CELERY ROOT tube root with knobbly brown skin, white flesh, and a celery-like flavor. Keep peeled celery root in acidulated water to stop it discoloring.

CHEESE

goat made from goat's milk, has an earthy, strong taste; available in both soft and firm textures, in various shapes and sizes, and sometimes rolled in ash or herbs.

gorgonzola a creamy Italian blue cheese with a mild, sweet taste; good as an accompaniment to fruit or used to flavor sauces (especially pasta).

haloumi a firm, cream-colored sheep-milk cheese matured in brine; haloumi can be grilled or fried, briefly, without breaking down. Should be eaten while still warm as it becomes tough and rubbery on cooling.

mascarpone an Italian fresh cultured-cream product made in much the same way as yogurt. Whiteish to creamy yellow in color, with a buttery-rich, luscious texture.

pecorino the Italian generic name for cheeses made from sheep milk; hard, white to pale-yellow in color. If you can't find it, use parmesan instead.

ricotta a soft, sweet, moist, white cow-milk cheese with a low fat content and a slightly grainy texture. The name roughly translates as "cooked again" and refers to ricotta's manufacture from a whey that is itself a by-product of other cheese making.

CHICKEN

breast fillet breast halved, skinned and boned.

drumette small fleshy part of the wing between shoulder and elbow, trimmed to resemble a drumstick.

drumstick leg with skin and bone intact.

small chicken also called a poussin; no more than 6 weeks old, weighing a maximum of 1 pound. Also a cooking term to describe splitting a small chicken open, flattening then grilling.

supremes breast with the skin on and wing bone still attached.

thigh skin and bone intact.

thigh cutlet thigh with skin and center bone intact; sometimes found skinned with bone intact.

thigh fillet thigh with skin and center bone removed.

CHICKPEAS (GARBANZO BEANS) an irregularly round, sandy-colored legume. Has a firm texture even after cooking, a floury mouth-feel, and robust nutty flavor; available canned or dried (soak for several hours in cold water before use).

CHILE generally, the smaller the chile, the hotter it is. Use rubber gloves when seeding and chopping fresh chiles as they can burn your skin. Removing seeds and membranes lessens the heat level.

CHOCOLATE, DARK (SEMISWEET) made of a high percentage of cocoa liquor and cocoa butter, and little added sugar. Dark chocolate is ideal in desserts and cakes.

CILANTRO also known as coriander, pak chee, or Chinese parsley; a bright-green leafy herb with a pungent flavor. Both stems and roots of cilantro can be used in cooking; wash well before using. Also available ground or as seeds; these should not be substituted for fresh as the flavors are completely different.

COCOA POWDER also called unsweetened cocoa; cocoa beans (cacao seeds) that have been fermented, roasted, shelled, ground into powder then cleared of most of the fat content.

COCONUT

cream obtained commercially from the first pressing of the coconut flesh alone, without the addition of water; the second pressing (less rich) is sold as coconut milk. Available in cans and cartons at most supermarkets.

flaked dried flaked coconut flesh.

milk not the liquid inside the fruit (coconut water), but the diluted liquid from the second pressing of the white flesh of a mature coconut. Available in cans and cartons at most supermarkets.

oil is extracted from the coconut flesh, so you don't get any of the fiber, protein, or carbohydrates present in the whole coconut. The best quality is virgin coconut oil, which is the oil pressed from the dried coconut flesh, and doesn't include the use of solvents or other refining processes.

sugar see Sugar

young are coconuts that are not fully mature. As a coconut ages, the amount of juice inside decreases, until it eventually disappears and is replaced by air.

CORNSTARCH available made from corn or wheat; used as a thickening agent in cooking.

COUSCOUS a fine, dehydrated, grain-like cereal product made from semolina; it swells to three or four times its original size when liquid is added. It is eaten like rice with a tagine, as a side dish or salad ingredient.

CREAM, POURING also called pure or fresh cream. It has no additives; minimum fat content varies by country.

CRÈME FRAÎCHE a mature, naturally fermented cream with a velvety texture and slightly tangy, nutty flavor. A French variation of sour cream, it can boil without curdling and be used in sweet and savory dishes.

CUMIN also known as zeera or comino; has a spicy, nutty flavor.

DAIKON also called white radish; this long, white horseradish has a wonderful, sweet flavor. After peeling, eat it raw in salads or shredded as a garnish; sliced or cubed and cooked in stir-fries and casseroles. The flesh is white but the skin can be white or black; buy those that are firm and unwrinkled from Asian food shops.

EDAMAME are fresh soy beans in the pod; available frozen from Asian food stores and well-stocked supermarkets.

EGGPLANT also called aubergine. Ranging in size from tiny to very large and in color from pale green to deep purple. Can also be purchased chargrilled, packed in oil, in jars.

FENNEL also known as finocchio or anise; a white to very pale green-white, firm, crisp, roundish vegetable. The bulb has a slightly sweet, anise flavor but the leaves have a much stronger taste. Also the name of dried seeds having a licorice flavor.

FISH SAUCE also called nam pla or nuoc nam; made from pulverized salted fermented fish, most often anchovies. Has a pungent smell and strong taste, so use sparingly.

FLOUR

all-purpose a general all-purpose wheat flour.

rice very fine, almost powdery, gluten-free flour; made from ground white rice. Used in baking, as a thickener, and in some Asian noodles and desserts. Another variety, made from glutinous sweet rice, is used for Chinese dumplings and rice paper.

self-rising plain flour sifted with baking powder in the proportion of 1 cup flour to 2 teaspoons baking powder.

whole-wheat milled with the wheat germ so it is higher in fiber and more nutritional than all-purpose flour.

FREEKEH is cracked roasted green wheat and can be found in well-stocked supermarkets, health-food, and specialty food stores.

GELATIN this recipes in this book call for powdered gelatin; it's also available in sheet form called leaf gelatin. One tablespoon of powdered gelatin is about the same as four gelatin sheets.

GINGER

glacé fresh ginger root preserved in sugar syrup; crystallized ginger (sweetened with cane sugar) can be used if rinsed with warm water and dried before using.

ground also called powdered ginger; used as a flavoring in baking but cannot be substituted for fresh ginger.

pickled pink or red colored; available, packaged, from Asian food markets. Pickled paper-thin shavings of ginger in a mixture of vinegar, sugar, and natural coloring; used in Japanese cooking.

HARISSA a Moroccan paste made from dried chiles, cumin, garlic, oil, and caraway seeds. Available from Middle Eastern food shops and well-stocked supermarkets.

LEMONGRASS a tall, clumping, lemon-smelling and -tasting, sharp-edged grass; the white part of the stem is used, finely chopped, in cooking.

MAPLE SYRUP, PURE distilled from the sap of sugar maple trees found only in Canada and the USA. Maple-flavored syrup or pancake syrup is not an adequate substitute for the real thing.

MUSHROOMS

cremini also called Swiss brown or roman mushrooms; are light brown mushrooms with a full-bodied flavor.

enoki clumps of long, spaghetti-like stems with tiny, white caps.

oyster also called abalone; grey-white mushrooms shaped like a fan. Prized for their smooth texture and subtle, oyster-like flavor. Also available pink.

porcini, dried also called cèpes; the richest-flavored mushrooms.

Expensive, but because they're so strongly flavored, only a small amount is required.

shiitake, fresh also known as Chinese black, forest, or golden oak mushrooms; although cultivated, they are large and meaty and have the earthiness and taste of wild mushrooms.

OIL

coconut see Coconut

olive made from ripened olives. Extra-virgin and virgin are the first and second press, respectively, of the olives; "light" refers to taste not fat levels.

peanut pressed from ground peanuts; most commonly used oil in Asian cooking because of its high smoke point (capacity to handle high heat without burning).

sesame made from toasted, crushed, white sesame seeds; used as a flavoring rather than a cooking oil.

ONION

green onion also called scallion; an immature onion picked before the bulb has formed. Has a long, bright-green edible stalk.

shallots also called French or golden shallots or eschalots; small and brown-skinned.

ORANGE BLOSSOM WATER concentrated flavoring made from orange blossoms.

PARCHMENT PAPER is a silicone-coated paper that is used for lining baking sheets and other pans so cooked food doesn't stick, making removal easy.

PERSIMMONS an autumnal fruit available in two varieties: an astringent one, eaten soft, and a non-astringent, or sweet, variety.

POMEGRANATE dark-red, leathery-skinned fruit about the size of an orange filled with hundreds of seeds, each wrapped in an edible lucent-crimson pulp with a unique tangy sweet-sour flavor.

POMEGRANATE MOLASSES not to be confused with pomegranate syrup or grenadine; pomegranate molasses is thicker, browner, and more concentrated in flavor—tart, sharp, slightly sweet and fruity. Available from Middle Eastern food stores or specialty food shops, and some supermarkets.

QUINOA pronounced *keen-wa*; is cooked and eaten as a grain alternative, but is in fact a seed. It has a delicate, slightly nutty taste and chewy texture, and is gluten-free.

RHUBARB a plant with long, green-red stalks; becomes sweet and edible when cooked.

RICE MALT SYRUP also known as brown rice syrup or rice syrup; is made by cooking brown rice flour with enzymes to break down its starch into sugars from which the water is removed.

ROSE WATER extract made from crushed rose petals, called gulab in India; used for its aromatic quality in sweetmeats and desserts.

SAFFRON available ground or in strands; imparts a yellow-orange color to food once infused. The quality can vary greatly; the best is the most expensive spice in the world.

SOY SAUCE several varieties are available in supermarkets and Asian food stores; use Japanese soy sauce unless stated otherwise.

SPINACH also called English spinach.

STAR ANISE dried star-shaped pod with an astringent aniseed flavor; used to flavor stocks and marinades. Available whole and ground, it is an essential ingredient in five-spice powder.

SUGAR

brown very soft, finely granulated sugar retaining molasses for its characteristic color and flavor.

coconut is not made from coconuts, but the sap of the blossoms of the coconut palm tree. The refined sap looks a little like raw or light brown sugar, and has a similar caramel flavor.

confectioners' also called powdered sugar; pulverized granulated sugar crushed together with a small amount of cornstarch.

granulated coarse, granulated table sugar.

palm also called nam tan pip, jaggery, jawa, or gula melaka; made from the sap of the sugar palm tree. Light brown to black in color and usually sold in rock-hard cakes; use brown sugar if unavailable.

superfine finely granulated table sugar.

SUMAC a purple-red, astringent spice, ground from berries growing on shrubs that flourish wild around the Mediterranean; adds a tart, lemony flavor. Available at most supermarkets.

SWISS CHARD a leafy green sometimes mistakenly called spinach.

TAHINI a rich, sesame-seed paste.

TAMARI a thick, dark soy sauce made mainly from soy beans, but without the wheat used in most standard soy sauces.

TOASTING desiccated coconut, pine nuts, and sesame seeds toast more evenly if stirred over low heat in a frying pan; their natural oils help turn them golden brown. Remove from pan immediately. Nuts and dried coconut can be toasted in the oven to release their essential oils. Spread them evenly onto a baking sheet then toast at 350°F for about 5 minutes.

TUSCAN KALE (CAVOLO NERO) has long, narrow, wrinkled leaves and a rich and astringent, mild cabbage flavor. It doesn't lose its volume like Swiss chard or spinach when cooked, but it does need longer cooking.

VANILLA

bean dried, long, thin pod from a tropical golden orchid; the minuscule black seeds inside the bean impart a luscious flavor in baking and desserts.

extract obtained from vanilla beans infused in water; a non-alcoholic version of essence.

paste made from vanilla beans and contains real seeds. Is highly concentrated: 1 teaspoon replaces a whole vanilla bean. Found in supermarkets in the baking section.

YOGURT, GREEK-STYLE plain yogurt strained in a cloth to remove the whey and to give it a creamy consistency.

Index

weldonowen

Published in North America by Weldon Owen
1045 Sansome Street, San Francisco, CA 94111
www.weldonowen.com
Weldon Owen is a division of Bonnier Publishing USA

This edition published in arrangement with Bauer Media Pty Limited. First
published in Australia in 2017 by Bauer Media Pty Limited under the title *Eat
Well Live Well: Wholefood Recipes by Colour for a Full Spectrum of Nutritional
Benefits*. © Bauer Media Pty Limited 2017. All rights reserved.

ISBN 978-1-68188-378-6

Library of Congress Cataloging-in-Publication data is available

Printed and bound in China

This edition printed in 2017

10 9 8 7 6 5 4 3 2 1